The Amazing Adventures of
Working Girl

9   8   7   6   5   4   3   2   1
Digit on the right indicates the number of this printing

Library of Congress Control Number: 2008942508

ISBN 978-0-7624-3348-3

Cover and interior design by Amanda Richmond
Edited by Jennifer Kasius
Typography: Franklin Gothic and American Typewriter

Running Press Book Publishers
2300 Chestnut Street
Philadelphia, PA 19103-4371

Visit us on the web!
www.runningpress.com

The Amazing Adventures of

Working Girl

**Real-Life Career Advice
You Can Actually Use**

Karen Burns

RUNNING PRESS
PHILADELPHIA · LONDON

Front Matter

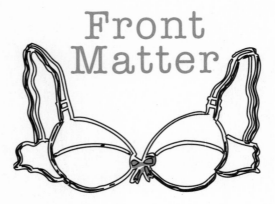

Who the heck is Working Girl

and where does she get off handing out career advice?

WORKING GIRL HAS HAD 59 JOBS OVER 40 YEARS IN 22 CITIES AND 4 COUNTRIES.

Working Girl got fired from only one of those jobs (and it wasn't her fault).

Working Girl has made a lot of mistakes. So you don't have to!

Here's the kind of stuff Working Girl (one person) has done:

- dug ditches in communist Czechoslovakia
- worked 19-hour shifts at Dunkin' Donuts (while also attending high school)
- got paid $50 an hour just for being American
- typed the same letter 535 times
- taught French generals how to lisp (not on purpose)
- modeled plus-sized bustiers
- got paid only $5 for 3 months of work (one of the mistakes)

Are you looking for a job? Do you have a job you hate? Are you afraid to quit your job and look for something better? Have you, God forbid, never had a job?

Take heart. Chin up. It's going to be okay—Working Girl is here to help. As you read this book, you'll laugh, learn, and feel a whole lot better about tackling the bewildering, weird, and wonderful world of work.

table of contents

Confident

Carefree

Appendices

How to
Read This Book

WORKING GIRL HOPES YOU ARE NOT READING THIS PAGE. She hopes you went straight to "Moonlighting" (page 72), or "Perverts at Work" (page 150), or "Friends" (page 196), or "Great Expectations" (page 51). Because this is the kind of book you open in the middle, read a chapter or two, say "Hmmmm," flip backward (or forward), read another few chapters, put it down, come back later, and read some more.

If you do decide to start at page one and keep going, you'll see that the 59 chapters correspond to Working Girl's 59 jobs and are arranged in three sections:

- Clueless. Simple yet important lessons learned the hard way.

- Confident. The basics (interviews, résumés, clothes, salary, networks, etc.).

- Carefree. Secrets to total job bliss.

Each and every chapter tells an excruciatingly true job tale and offers advice based on that tale. The chapters are not in chronological order by job. That would be boring. Besides, we can be confident when we're 18. Turn clueless at 25. Discover carefree at 33. Slip back to clueless for a spell. Then get confident again. Working Girl did. You will, too.

Have fun.

CLUELESS

Stress Test

CONTRARY TO WHAT YOU MIGHT THINK, the jobs with the highest stress levels are the ones with the least amount of responsibility and pay.

An illustration: When Working Girl was 12 she earned $1.25 an hour cleaning house for Mr. and Mrs. Fox, a sweet 80-something couple living next door. Every Tuesday afternoon she vacuumed, dusted, scrubbed, windexed, swept, and polished their one-bedroom apartment.

You'd think this job would've been simple. But there was one big problem: As far as Working Girl could tell, Mr. and Mrs. Fox's apartment was never dirty.

It looked the same after she'd cleaned it as before.

Each week, your eager-to-please-yet-still-clueless heroine rearranged knickknacks to show she had dusted, grooved the carpet with vacuum cleaner marks to show she had vacuumed, and switched the position of pillows to show she had fluffed. Is that what Mr. and Mrs. Fox wanted? Working Girl never really knew. They never commented one way or another. And of course, back then, WG was too wussy to ask.

Yup, despite her tender years, Working Girl had achieved Level 6 on the Work Stress-O-Meter (see right). How did this happen? Because:

Stress Comes from Feeling Powerless

You may have a challenging, demanding, busy, even at times overwhelming job, *but* if you have a sense of power over it, you will be able to handle the stress.

Where does this sense of power come from? At a minimum, you need to:

- enjoy the work
- feel able to do, or learn to do, the work
- be given the resources you need
- be able to see results, and
- be recognized for those results.

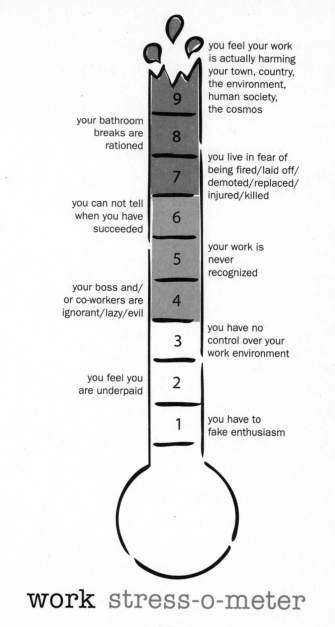

you feel your work is actually harming your town, country, the environment, human society, the cosmos

your bathroom breaks are rationed

you live in fear of being fired/laid off/demoted/replaced/injured/killed

you can not tell when you have succeeded

your work is never recognized

your boss and/or co-workers are ignorant/lazy/evil

you have no control over your work environment

you feel you are underpaid

you have to fake enthusiasm

9
8
7
6
5
4
3
2
1

work stress-o-meter

Yeah, it's also nice to get a good salary, work with people you like, set your own hours, and have a bit of job security.

But the five points above are the essential formula for a happy work life.

Easier said than done, you say.

Read on, dear fellow working girls, and learn how to get happy and love your job.

JOB SURVIVAL TIP

Susan, ADMINISTRATIVE ASSISTANT

"I work at a computer all day. When I just can't stand the stress of sitting there another minute, I go to the ladies' room and do fifty jumping jacks. It gets my blood flowing again. People wonder why I always come out of the bathroom all pink and breathless!"

cigarette girl

Miss Manners

YOUR BOSS NEVER SAYS "PLEASE." Customers call you "Hey You." Co-workers interrupt you while you're on the phone, borrow your supplies without asking, and steal your lunch out of the fridge. What do you do? You deploy the secret weapon of every working girl: etiquette.

Etiquette?

Yup. Etiquette is more than just the social graces. It's a powerful tool. It can be used to control people and situations.

Example: In high school Working Girl had a part-time job minding the cigarette counter at the corner drugstore.

The worst part? The leathery 50-something men with yellowed fingers who came in every night for their Marlboros or Lucky Strikes. They reeked, they winked, they leered, and they called her "Babe." If she hadn't been standing behind a chest-high countertop, they would have pinched her, too.

Working Girl was sorta scared of these men but tolerated them until one evening enough was finally enough, and she got up the nerve to try something new. Two minutes into her shift, the first customer shuffled up.

She took a deep breath, lifted her chin, looked him in the eye, and said in a loud-but-pleasant voice, "Good evening, sir. May I help you, sir?"

The customer wore a mullet and a T-shirt that read, I'M WITH STUPID. He was clearly a winker and a Babe-er, and had probably never been addressed as "sir" in his entire life.

"Uh," he said.

Working Girl would have bet a week's pay he'd been just about to mumble "Apackamarlborosbabe." Instead he removed the cigarette from his mouth and said, "May I have a pack of Marlboros, please, miss?" No Babe. No wink.

Do you want to stand out from the crowd? Do you

want people to treat you with respect?

Say please and thank you, smile, shake hands, look people in the eye, learn to pronounce their names correctly (ask them how!), listen with interest, be punctual, and take five minutes to write a thank-you note. You know, the basics.

Etiquette puts people at ease and makes life run more smoothly. Etiquette shows people that you expect them to treat you as well as you treat them. And it's free.

Are you feeling guilty about all the times you've been less than perfectly polite? Never mind. Good manners do not come naturally to anyone. From this point on, please learn, and do, the basics.

The workplace has its own basic business etiquette. It's not complicated. Start with Working Girl's Daily Dozen and stand back. The results will amaze you:

#1 Introduce yourself with your first and last name. Shake hands firmly.

#2 Say "good morning/afternoon," not "hi."

#3 When introducing/emailing people, start with the name of the senior person.

#4 Don't shake hands across a desk or table (stand up and walk around).

#5 Regardless of gender, the first person to reach a door opens it.

#6 Regardless of gender, the person nearest the elevator door gets off first.

#7 Treat everyone the same—well.

#8 Thank people.

#9 Praise sincerely.

#10 If you hear gossip, instantly forget it (don't spread it).

#11 Even at boring meetings, show some interest.

#12 Don't wear a gallon of perfume, or bring smelly foods for lunch.

It's truly as simple as: Treat other people with respect and other people will treat you with respect.

If they don't—if they still call you names, interrupt you, or swipe your lunch, you have another problem entirely (see "Hell Is Other People," page 201).

filing mouse

Growing a Spine

THE OFFICE. Chances are good you have worked, are working, or will work in one.

Working Girl got her first office job the summer she was 12. At 12 you work so cheap it doesn't matter if you are unqualified. And Working Girl was.

She couldn't type. She couldn't take shorthand.* She couldn't even answer the phone because she had such a teensy little voice no one could hear her.

But she did know the alphabet, so she spent the long, hot days filing. Which she hated, of course. On

---

* People really did take shorthand back then.

the bright side, it left her plenty of energy to hide.

Yup, Working Girl was shy. So shy that when Boss Man barged in every morning at 8 and boomed, "Good morning!" she could answer with only a little squeak. Her transition from home life, where you are pretty much loved for yourself, to work life, where you are loved for what you can do, was brutal. Her co-workers had no idea how terrified she was.

One fateful day, Working Girl and Boss Man were alone in the office. The worst happened. BM spoke to her.

"Is there any more coffee?" he said.

Working Girl, who did not drink coffee, didn't know. But the percolator (this being pre–Mr. Coffee) was in fact empty.

"Would you make some more?" he asked.

Working Girl had never made coffee before, but, naturally, she was too chicken to admit it. So she got up and took the percolator from his hands.

"Great," said BM, "bring me a cup when it's ready."

Working Girl had often watched her mother operate a percolator. So she discarded the used grounds. She filled the pot with water up to the brown stain mark. She filled the filter with Maxwell House. She plugged the thing in. It sighed and began to gurgle.

When the gurgling stopped, Working Girl poured what she prayed would be coffee into a mug and took it to BM, just as she had seen his secretary do.

He took a sip. Then he slammed his fist down on the desk.

"Where did you learn to make coffee, young lady?" he demanded.

"Eeep," said Working Girl.

"This is the best cuppa joe I've ever tasted!" BM thundered. "From now on, you're making all the coffee around here!"

Working Girl was horrified. But she was put in charge of the percolator for the rest of the summer. And eventually was able to make coffee without wanting to go home and hide under the bed.

Dear reader, Working Girl devoutly hopes that you never feel as inadequate as she did. But she suspects that sometimes you fear that you just can't manage what's being asked of you. Don't we all? Of course, like you, she's always heard that confidence comes from believing in yourself. That's what the experts say.

But, she wonders, what if you don't believe in yourself? What then? Can you go to a store and buy confidence? Can you go online and download it?

No, but you can get it another way: By accomplishing something. Even a small thing. Like making coffee.

Or, nowadays, keeping the Starbucks order straight.

JOB SURVIVAL TIP

Karen, TECHNICAL WRITER

"I keep a running list of my accomplishments in a text file on my desktop. Whenever I do something worth remembering, I open up that file and jot it down, with the date. When the time comes for my yearly review, or when I want to revise my résumé, I go into this file. It's very handy. I know I would not remember a lot of this stuff otherwise!"

store clerk

Fear & Loathing

WORK. UGH.

Working Girl truly, madly, deeply hated her first 21 jobs.[*] Example: clerk in the books section of a department store.

She should have enjoyed it, because she loves books, but . . . the mind-numbing, soul-destroying tedium! No customers, no duties, not even a co-worker around to talk to. Reading the books was, of course, forbidden.

Here's how it went: Punch in at 6 p.m. Take up post

---

[*] Nor was she so hot about her next 29 jobs. In fact, she didn't love a job until #52.

behind cash register. Straighten bookmarks. Wander around. Flip through bestsellers on front table. Gnaw on hangnail. Reflect: "Wouldn't the world be a better place if food and shelter and cute clothes were free?" Check watch: 6:01. Repeat until 9 p.m.

What to do when you hate hate hate your job?

Consider this fact: The probability of you leaving any job is precisely 100%. Really. You are positively absolutely going to leave that job, whether you quit, are fired, retire, or die.

So, given that you *are* going to leave the job you hate, you have two decisions to make:

#1 When will you leave?

#2 What are you going to do until you leave?

You are in the driver's seat. Don't be like Working Girl—take control of your life!

So set a deadline. Whether it's tomorrow or a year from now, identifying a clear cutoff point to the crummy job will help.

Then decide on how you're going to act in the meantime. Here are some tricks:

- Find a thing you *do* like about the job. Even if it's only the tapioca they serve in the cafeteria or the fact that the walls are a nice shade of white, focusing on the positive will make you happier.

- Every day, do something that brings you closer to

being able to say, "I quit." Save five bucks. Take a class to qualify for a new job. Update your résumé.

- Do something nice for yourself before you go into work. Put blueberries on your cereal. Plug in your iPod and dance around the house in your underwear. Stop for a double latte with chocolate sprinkles.

- No matter how much you hate the job, give fair labor for your pay. It's good for your self-respect. And you may find that the work seems less horrible. Tip: Identify the hardest part of the job and do that thing first. The rest of the day will feel easier in comparison.

- After hours, explore healthy ways to vent stress: See a friend, exercise, redesign your Facebook page, go dancing, take in a movie.

In other words: Don't stew, do!

JOB SURVIVAL TIP

Rachel, THERAPIST

"My first job was clerical and I hated it. Without even realizing, I stopped caring about my hair or what I wore. I started being late to work for no good reason. Unsurprisingly, I was soon fired. Today when I notice that I'm becoming habitually tardy or starting to slob around in sweatpants a lot, I know it's a sign of self-sabotage and that something bigger is wrong."

seamstress

Picky Picky Picky

ONE SUMMER, WORKING GIRL'S BOSS (she worked at a fabric shop at the time) let her have a bolt of unbleached muslin for nothing. Always looking for ways to scare up a few extra bucks, she decided to take that bolt of muslin and sew and sell halter tops.

To make them look less boringly beige, she embroidered the fronts with flowers, ferns, and butterflies. Hopes high, she took her creations to the local hippie boutique. The manager fingered the cheap fabric and glanced at the hand embroidery. "Where did you get these designs?" she asked.

"I drew them myself," said Working Girl.

"Your art is insufficiently complex," the manager said. "These will never sell."

Everyone's a critic. And it's hard not to take criticism personally. No matter who you are or what your work is, criticism always feels like someone just ran over your new puppy with a Hummer.

So when you are criticized—as, sooner or later, you will be—your first action should be a nonaction. That's right. At the meeting where your presentation is panned, at the annual review where you are told you're not cutting it, you should say this and only this: *"Thank you. Let me think about your comments and get back to you."*

Then smile, look the person in the eye, and leave.

When you get home, feel free to let your emotions all hang out. Cry, whine, rant. Do fifty jumping jacks. Watch a mindless sitcom.

CRITICISM DON'TS

· Don't ignore it.

· Don't make excuses.

· Don't get visibly angry.

· Don't attack your criticizer.

· Don't let it make you timid.

· Don't obsess.

Once you've got that out of your system and you're still at home in your bunny slippers, answer this question: Was the criticism accurate? Be honest.

Way more than half the time, the criticism is going to be justified in some way (if not, see box below). Say, for example, your criticizer complained you didn't do X. Maybe you didn't know you were supposed to do X, you tried to do X but failed, you disagree X is the right thing to do, or you just hate to do X. But if X was your job and you didn't do it well, you need to recognize the problem. And fix it.

CRITICISM IFS

If the criticism is unfounded:

Analyze it with the same logic you use for justified criticism. Then say: *"I have considered your remarks about X. To the best of my knowledge, I have done X! Please help me understand where you believe I have gone wrong."*

If the criticizer has an evil agenda and is just trying to hurt you:

You should still consider whether the criticism was accurate. It's possible! If so, fix the problem. If not, proceed as for unfounded criticism (above).

The following day, or as soon as possible, go see your criticizer. Say this: "I thought about what you said and I recognize that I did fail to do X. Here are some ways I've come up with to correct the problem. What do you think? Do you have anything to add?"

Then stop talking. Do not belabor your point. Do not apologize a million times. Focus on the solution, not the problem.

Your criticizer will be blown away. You'll have shown yourself to be the rare human being who can take criticism and learn from it. It's a very cool skill that requires lots of practice. Don't despair if you can't pull it off the first time, or even the tenth time.

Finally, consider that the problem may be your criticizer. He/she may be inept, dishonest, distracted, or flakey—i.e., not qualified to be handing out critiques of other people's work.

Example: When Working Girl was told her embroidery designs were insufficiently complex, she took her halter tops and started to slink away, crushed.

The manager stopped her. "I'll tell you what," she said, "I'll take them on a trial basis."

Thrilled, Working Girl handed over her entire inventory and started to imagine what she would do with the extra cash from her sales. Two weeks later she returned to the boutique. It was gone.

The building was still there, but everything inside—

including Working Girl's halter tops—had disappeared. A handwritten sign on the door said, "Gone Bankrupt."

cashier

Praise Be

WE LOVE TO BE LOVED.

Which is why Working Girl volunteered one July to paint the employee break room at the drugstore where she cashiered. On her own time. Even though that summer she was working two jobs. Jobs she commuted to on her bicycle. In 112-degree heat. Did she mention the jobs were in neighboring towns 10 miles apart? They were.

So, yes, Working Girl was expecting that her fabulous work ethic would earn her a raise or praise or ... something.

The project took two weeks. No one offered to help, but Working Girl didn't mind (more glory for *her!*). When she finished, the break room was fresh and clean and no longer smelled like cigarette smoke.

Everyone was thrilled, right? Um, wrong. Her boss, who had been reluctant to give permission for the paint job in the first place, said nothing. Her co-workers were resentful and suspicious and disparaging. No one actually came out and said so, but everyone probably felt that Working Girl's ambition and energy made them look like slobs by comparison.

Still. Would it have killed them to show a little appreciation?

Here's what Working Girl learned from this incident:

Do not rely on praise from others.

Praise, recognition, appreciation—those are drugs. Actual drugs. When you're praised your brain releases dopamine, a chemical that transmits pleasure signals, the same chemical released by cocaine.

And you know what? No matter how much praise you get, you can always use a little more. No one ever feels over-appreciated.

Another thing: You'll notice as you pursue your career that the good job you do quickly becomes regarded as "business as usual." In fact, sometimes it seems as if only failure gets attention. It's the pits, but it's human nature.

That's why smart working girls reward *themselves* for a job well done. Think about what success means to you (see "How to Tell When You Are Successful," page 236). Look for satisfaction in things you can see, judge, measure, and evaluate. Set personal standards, and when you satisfy those standards, feel good inside your little old self. Maybe even reward yourself with a small treat—a new CD, a movie with friends.

All of this is not to say that praise, when it comes, won't feel just peachy. It will. But don't be a dope. Remember the dopamine. Don't get addicted to praise.

R-E-S-P-E-C-T
and How to Get It

HONEST WORK, BE IT EVER SO HUMBLE, DESERVES
RESPECT.

It's hard to remember that when you're wearing a
hairnet, scraping uneaten food off dirty plates, and
stacking said plates into an industrial-size dishwasher.

It's harder when you're 13 and recently enrolled at
a new school, and the dirty plates belong to your
classmates.

It's even harder when the reason you're working in
the school cafeteria is so that you qualify for the free

lunch program—not even because your family is poor, but because your mother believes it's a good way to teach you responsibility.

Note to Working Girl's mother: Washing dishes at Emerson Elementary School did not teach her the value of a dollar, develop her work ethic, or show her that there is no such thing as a free lunch.* What she discovered was that if you count on getting your self-respect from your position in society, you may be in for a big disappointment.

Since those days, Working Girl has learned that:

Respect is not something you can pursue.

Nope, it's a by-product of other things that you pursue. Namely, integrity, candor, trustworthiness, excellence, decency—you know, being a Good Person. Respect from other people is a result of your good character. Simple, huh?

You will occasionally run across a person who—despite your fabulosity—does not treat you with respect. Maybe he/she is insecure, paranoid, immature, or jealous. Who knows?

Do these two things:

#1 Recognize that *something is wrong with that person.*

#2 Go on with your life as if the problem person is not even there.

---

* What it did do was ground her in the beginnings of self-reliance. Maybe WG's mom was a feminist without knowing it.

Of course, if the problem person is your boss or a co-worker whose performance you rely on, the situation can get sticky.

So here's what Working Girl does: She refers to her handy 3x3 Respect-O-Graph. It reminds her of what's real and where her power lies.

Your powerful behavior may fix the problem. Or it may not (not all situations are salvageable). But you will have your *own* respect. Which is the most important thing.

Working Girl's
3x3 respect-o-graph

(do any or all, in any combination)

Tell yourself every day	Do away from work	Do at work
"This is not personal."	Vent! (To friends, family, your cat.)	Be charming. (Never underestimate the power of your own charm.)
"I have more power than I think I do."	Journal! (A problem on paper feels more manageable.)	Be distant. (Ignore the problem person as much as possible.)
"This person may never give me the respect I deserve, and that's okay."	Get help! (From a job coach, clergyman, counselor, or other pro.)	Be cool. (Don't let them see they are getting to you.)

LeAnn, "ADMIN"

"I have two master's degrees, one in anthropology and one in public health. But while my kids are small I'm working as a part-time admin for my church. I had been warned but I was still surprised at how differently people treated me once I became 'just' an office worker. So I decided to treat it all as an interesting anthropological study. I watch their behavior and tell myself, 'How quaint. How amusing.'"

Anger Management

Five-year-olds run fast. They don't get tired. They can scoot under hedges without ducking. They aren't slowed down by, say, looking both ways when crossing a street.

So by the time Working Girl caught up to little Marcie, she'd run 14 blocks. In flip-flops. In 110-degree heat.

"I told you to stop!" she panted, grabbing the child and collapsing onto a patch of Bermuda grass under a palm tree.

Working Girl was 15 and too young to nanny 3 kids, 12 hours a day, 5 days a week, plus cooking, cleaning, and laundry. But she did. Salary: 25 cents an hour.

"You're getting a spanking!" Working Girl snarled, and lifted her hand to administer a couple swats to Marcie's backside. (Standard procedure in those days. Don't judge!)

She stopped. "What's that?" It was a red mark, that was clear enough, on the back of this little person's thigh. But it had a funny shape. It looked exactly like a . . . belt buckle.

"Where did you get this mark?" Working Girl asked.

"From Daddy," said the little girl.

Working Girl's fury dissolved. No spanking that day, or any day.

Anger is scary. And it's around us every day. At work, too. Wherever you find anger, it comes in two varieties: Yours. Theirs.

Yours: It's okay to feel anger. What's not okay is to express it in destructive ways. Of course you know this. The problem is what to do in the heat of the moment.

What you do is stop. Whatever you're doing, stop it. Inhale. Exhale. Are your fists clenched, your shoulders hunched? Unclench and unhunch. Repeat.

Express your anger only when you can do it unemotionally. Use a normal conversational tone. Attack the problem, not the person. Summarize what made you angry, and state how the situation could be made better for you.

It only sounds simple. It's not. It takes practice and effort. But the mark of a mature person is to be able to feel an emotion without acting on it. So keep trying!

Theirs: At some point you will work with people who can't control their anger or, worse, who try to use their anger to control you. Of course, if it's violent anger just get out of there. But most workplace anger is verbal and in passing. It may even be part of your job to deal with frequently angry people. In any case, it pays to develop a system. Here's Working Girl's. It has seven pretty simple steps:

- First, adopt an unemotional, bland attitude.

- Second, don't talk much. Listen.

- Third, look for common ground. Agree where possible.

- Fourth, as the person winds down, start identifying the issues.

- Fifth, list the issues on a sheet of paper.

- Sixth, ask for ideas for resolving the issues. Write those down, too.

- Seventh, ask for help in creating a list of problems, solutions, and action items.

Congratulations. You've turned a freaked-out rant into a dull-as-dirt business meeting.

Standing up to an angry person takes courage, but if you can do it constructively, as per above, you will be powerful and most people will hesitate to dump on you. Try it and see.

What happened with Marcie and her two brothers? Working Girl nannied them all summer, the family moved away, and she never saw or heard from them again. But she still wonders whatever became of that little girl.

P.S. Sometimes humor, wit, or irony (never sarcasm) can defuse an angry situation. It's risky, though. Only try it if you are truly funny.

Christmas temp

The
Grand Illusion

"WOULD YOU LIKE TO STAY ON?"

"Pardon?"

"Would you like to stay on as a permanent employee after Christmas?"

Working Girl set down the box of red shiny ornaments she'd been emptying. "Doing what?"

"Stocking. You could eventually work your way up to cashier. Maybe even management. This is a good company to work for."

"Hmmm," said Working Girl. Stay at Rexall Drugs permanently? As in, the rest of her life? It was what Bob and Dan and Anita and Joyce, her co-workers, were doing.

"Sure, it isn't the most exciting job," Bob added, "but you'd have security."

Security. Do you think Working Girl should have stuck with Rexall? Heck, by now she could have worked her way up to district manager!

Or not. Because there's only one thing you need to know about security, and that is that it doesn't exist. Security is the loosiest and goosiest of feelings. You can feel secure when you're not at all. You can feel insecure when you're really quite safe.

Anyway, we are never one hundred percent secure. It ain't possible. That's why a life built around the quest for security is a sad kind of life.

So if at some point you're tempted to "settle for a sure thing," a thing you wouldn't otherwise want, remember this: What may look like a safe easy path now is just a big fat lie. Nothing, not hard work, not education, not seniority, not connections—nothing—guarantees your continued employment at a particular company.

And when you think about it, security is just another way of saying that there's nothing else left that can happen to you. How gloomy. How boring. Taking

chances (*smart* chances—see "Looking and
Leaping," page 176) is essential to growth and fulfill-
ment and happiness and life.

The only real security is the security you carry
around inside you.

No surprise ending here: Working Girl left Rexall
right after Christmas.

> **ETERNAL TRUTH**
> Life is supposed to be a little bit dangerous.

The
Big Picture

HERE'S A SHORT, SAD TALE OF A FAILURE TO COM-
MUNICATE. In Paris,[*] Working Girl got hired to write
a brochure for a small international insurance firm. It
shoulda been simple—interview the president, write a
draft, get feedback, tweak, voilà. Three weeks, four
pages, tops.

Except. After five interviews and six drafts, the
president still did not feel the brochure text reflected
the grandeur and complexity of his business.

[*] Yup, Working Girl worked overseas for a while. Keep reading!

"You make our work sound so simple," he said, frowning.

Working Girl thought, but did not say, *It's insurance. How hard can it be?*

But the president was so mired down in minutiae he was incapable of seeing the big picture. That brochure never did get finished. Fact: Very few people understand their work from a global perspective.

- Want to stand out from the crowd?
- Want to make your job tons more interesting?
- Want to be hugely more effective in that job?

Take the trouble and time to learn how your company and what it does fits into the overall industry, the country, the planet. It's fun. Here's how:

Don't Drink the Kool-Aid

When you're trying to understand the business you're working in, do not depend solely on sources inside your company. Training courses, orientation manuals, company newsletters have all been spun to reflect the party line and are often written by clueless PR types (Working Girl knows—she was one). Read business magazines, newspapers, books. Someone smart is probably blogging about your industry. Get in on the conversation. Are there consumer or special interest groups that criticize your company? Find out what they're saying.

Disregard the Rocket Scientists

When you study any task, process, or business, do it from the mind-set of "How can I make this simple and clear?" Ask questions. If you don't understand the answers, ask again. Some people want you to believe their work is intricate and mysterious and way over your head. Don't fall for it. Nothing is impossible to understand. Not even rocket science.

Give It the Kid Test

When you think you've got a handle on the big picture, try explaining your industry and what you do in it to an intelligent 12-year-old willing to listen. Do the kid's eyes glaze over? You are not doing a good job of explaining. If you can't describe what your company does in three minutes or less, you don't really understand it.

Some people are naturally big-picture people. Some are detail oriented. Detail types will find this chapter a difficult (even annoying) assignment. But it's important to step back, identify, and understand your work's place in the world.

· It will make you a better big-picture person.

· It will make you a better detail person.

· It will just plain make you better at what you do.

ditchdigger

Great Expectations

WORKING GIRL ONCE HAD A JOB WITHOUT KNOWING IT. She'd originally signed up for volunteer work in communist Czechoslovakia. Her plan: A little philanthropy, a lotta fun.

Surprise #1: The "philanthropy" was digging a ditch.

Surprise #2: The ditch was on top of a mountain.

After a week of mountain climbing and ditch digging, Working Girl and her fellow volunteers (soft capitalist types—French, American, Dutch) started knocking off work around 3. Then 2. Then before noon.

Surprise #3: The boss reduced our food rations.

What we conscripts—er, volunteers—did not know was that the boss's boss, known as The Engineer, was keeping track of the hours we worked. Each hour corresponded to some (small) amount of money. That was the money allotted to buy our groceries. Bottom line: The less we worked, the less we ate.

We were outraged. We stopped all work entirely. Our total rations were reduced to tea and bread. We wrote a formal letter of protest. Nothing happened. We wrote another letter of protest. Finally, The Engineer came to meet with us and, after much haggling, a compromise was reached: We would perform more work (less than The Engineer wanted) and he would supply more food (less than we wanted).

Expectations are everything. We volunteers expected an enriching cultural experience and the satisfaction of having helped the world. Our communist boss expected free labor to get his ditch dug.

When you find yourself disappointed or otherwise unpleasantly surprised, it's because reality did not measure up to your expectations. It's amazing how often this happens. When you complain, you are told to "manage your expectations," but no one tells you how.

Here's how:

The more you know about a thing—a process, a person, a place—the better you are able to predict outcomes. Knowledge really is power. So before you commit to a job or any project, do your research. Talk to people with experience in the area. Read. Think back to when you've dealt with similar situations. Apply common sense (you know, the old "If it sounds too good to be true, it probably is").

Another thing about expectations: We don't always know what ours are. Many expectations are unconscious. So ask yourself, "What do I really want? What is my real agenda?" Share it with some smart people and get their reactions.

> **ETERNAL TRUTH**
> Unmet unconscious expectations are the source of much unhappiness.

Some say the key to avoiding disappointment is low expectations, but Working Girl is not so cynical. She says the key to avoiding disappointment is *realistic* expectations.

One thing you should always expect: That you will in some way be surprised. Nothing ever turns out *exactly* the way you think it's going to. That's what makes life such a cool adventure.

Donnette, HAIRSTYLIST

"Hair is so important! Clients often have a vision for their hair that they aren't able to describe. Or they want a style that isn't realistic for their particular hair. This is why I never overbook. I take the time to listen to what the client wants and then to explain what is possible for me to deliver, and how and why. People appreciate the information. A client who knows what to expect is a better and happier client. With prettier hair."

researcher

When You Bomb

YOU ARE WONDERFUL. YOU REALLY ARE. You have a special gift to give to the world that only you can give.

You will from time to time completely and utterly botch things up.

Oh yes.

You will fail.

Like the time Working Girl accepted an assignment to research French regulations on organic monomers. No, she has no idea what monomers are, organic or otherwise. Scientific background? None. Legal knowledge? Nada. French fluency? Not good enough by far. But she spent a month slogging through legal and scientific texts, in French, and then—by any standard—wrote the world's lamest and most pathetic and most useless "report."[*]

Of course, Working Girl had no business taking this job in the first place. Sure, it seemed like a good idea at the time, and as usual she was in dire need of the money. But she shoulda said, "Sorry, no, I am not qualified."

That's the thing with failure, you can always see later where you went wrong and why it was a bad idea from the get-go.

Failure is salvageable if we learn from our mistakes. So when (not if) you bomb, here are a couple tips:

- Reassess your strengths and weaknesses (see "The Right Stuff," page 180).

- Consider if the work is something you truly want to learn. If so, try again in a different and smarter way (see "The Persistence Loop," page 170).

Oh, and do not neglect to admit your error, take responsibility for it, and if possible make reparations (see "Do the Right Thing," page 69).

---

[*] What did the clients think? Well, they paid her. But they never hired her again.

Once all that is done, you may feel better. You may not. Please try to accept that sometimes a screw-up is just a screw up. That what you attempted was simply a bad idea, doomed from the start. You will know this if afterward you say, "What was I *thinking*?"

Forgive yourself. Learn what you can learn. Then walk away, baby. Do not look back.

JOB SURVIVAL TIP

Amanda, WRITER, BICYCLE SALESWOMAN, WAITRESS

"I feel my failures big. When I suffer any kind of setback, I go home, cry, take a bath, let myself mourn and be miserable. I'm not one of those stiff-upper-lip people! But then I get over it fast. I bounce back, move on to the next thing, a thing that energizes and excites me. I might take lessons from the failure. But I never focus on the past."

Your Paycheck Bounces ...
and Other Signs You Need to Quit Your Job

EVERY JOB HAS UPSIDES AND DOWNSIDES.

Working Girl moonlighted as a hostess in a steak-house for a while. Upside: She was allowed to eat a baked potato for every shift she worked. Downside: Part of her job was to evict the homeless people who snuck into the ladies' room to crash on the couch at night.

But an even worse downside came on her first payday. Instead of handing her a check, her boss handed her a line: "We can't pay you because we lost your W-2." Two weeks later, it was, "The checks were delayed in the mail." Two weeks after that: "The accountant is in the hospital and couldn't do the payroll."

Eight weeks into the job, Working Girl received her first paycheck. It bounced. She didn't get any money until she complained to the National Labor Relations Board. And by then, of course, she had found another job.

Some job downsides you can put up with. Others— not so much. If you are wondering if it's time to move up and out of your job, take this test:

Signs You Need to Quit Your Job

1. You are asked to do something illegal or unethical.	Yes	No
2. Your company is losing customers or losing money.	Yes	No
3. You get lousy (or no) raises.	Yes	No
4. Your boss doesn't bother to learn your name.	Yes	No
5. Your style doesn't match their style.	Yes	No
6. You find it hard to get out of bed in the morning.	Yes	No
7. You spend more time on "red tape" than on your actual work.	Yes	No
8. You feel tired by 10 a.m.	Yes	No
9. You call in sick when you aren't sick.	Yes	No
10. Your boss is emotionally abusive.	Yes	No

11. Your values are at odds with the company's values.   Yes   No

12. You have started smoking, or are drinking more than you should/want.   Yes   No

13. Your duties change (not for the better).   Yes   No

14. You cry on the way to or from work.   Yes   No

15. You have been demoted.   Yes   No

16. You are taken for granted.   Yes   No

17. You aren't promoted because the company "needs you where you are."   Yes   No

18. You slept with a co-worker (or boss) and it ended badly.   Yes   No

19. Your workload doubled and your pay remained the same.   Yes   No

20. You quit exercising or spending time with loved ones.   Yes   No

21. Your boss set you up to take the blame for someone else's error.   Yes   No

22. You are no longer invited to relevant meetings.   Yes   No

23. You are not copied on messages central to your job.   Yes   No

24. You gain, or lose, a lot of weight.   Yes   No

25. You hate your boss.   Yes   No

26. Your boss hates you.   Yes   No

27. You are underpaid.   Yes   No

28. You work overtime for weeks at a stretch (and you don't want to).   Yes   No

29. Your job turned out to be not what was promised.   Yes   No

30. You aren't learning anything new.	Yes	No
31. You see no room for advancement.	Yes	No
32. Your co-workers are racist, obscene, incompetent, bullying backstabbers.	Yes	No
33. You know you are doing a bad job and you don't care.	Yes	No
34. You are not getting enough sleep, or you are sleeping too much.	Yes	No
35. You have no friends outside of work.	Yes	No

If you answered "yes" to more than 15 of these (although some are deal breakers all by themselves), it's time for a change.

Go directly to "Quitting with Class," page 130.

Shafted

HOW'S THIS FOR IRONY: Working Girl freelanced in Europe for three years and the only client who cheated her was a fellow American.

Let us call her L.G.

From the start Working Girl didn't much like L.G. She was witchy. When L.G. visited Paris she was so rude to waiters, store clerks, and hotel keepers that WG was embarrassed to be seen with her.

But L.G. gave Working Girl her very first magazine writing assignment. Working Girl was thrilled; she was finally a real writer! The job, an article on health care for Americans in Paris, was fun to research and write. She finished it fast and mailed it to L.G., who was based in New Jersey, and L.G. mailed her a check.

So far, so good. A month later L.G. phoned. "I'd like you to do the same thing for housing," she said.

"I'd love to," chirped Working Girl. Ten days later she sent the finished article to Jersey.

Weeks passed. Working Girl sent L.G. a postcard ("Did you get my story?"). No reply. Then a letter. Nothing. She phoned. The number was no longer in service.

Had L.G. gone out of business? Had she been run over by a bus? Had a family member fallen ill? Yup, Working Girl wasted energy worrying about L.G.'s well-being.

You know the ending. Despite numerous phone calls and letters (this was pre-email), Working Girl never heard from L.G. and never got paid.[*] In the end she decided to feel lucky that in all her years freelancing she's been stiffed only once.

The good news is that most employers will not cheat you. Which is not to say there aren't bad people out there. There are. Your job is to learn to avoid them. Here's how:

- **Be intuitive.** Don't be like Working Girl, who ignored her misgivings about L.G.

---

[*] However, while writing this book, Working Girl googled L.G. There she was, still in business, still publishing the same magazine. Hey, L.G.! You owe WG $450!

- **Be shrewd.** The cliché holds: If it looks too good to be true, it probably is.

- **Be cautious.** Ask around. Research the reputation of a potential client or boss.

- **Be organized.** Keep good records of hours you've worked, jobs you've done, vacation and comp time accrued, etc.

- **Be businesslike.** A reputable client won't be offended if you ask for 50 percent up front; an honest employer will not blink at giving you the details of an offer in writing.

- **Be honest yourself.** Integrity is contagious.

But what if, despite your precautions, you get shafted anyway? It happens. Here is what to do, in the order in which you should do it:

- **Step One:** Stop working for The Shafter right away. Do not continue to deliver goods and/or services, hoping for the best. Go find honest people to work for.

- **Step Two:** Ask The Shafter, clearly and politely, to give you what you're owed. Appeal to The Shafter's better nature, allowing room for doing the right thing while saving face.

- **Step Three:** Be persistent. The Shafter may pay you just to get rid of you.

- **Step Four:** Go to a superior, if The Shafter has one. Go to a professional association, if that applies. Go to the law, if it makes fiscal sense.

- **Step Five:** If you have done *everything you can* and The Shafter still has not paid up, let it go. You don't want the experience to ruin your love for your work or to make you fearful of trusting people.

ETERNAL TRUTH

Don't let the occasional rotten egg ruin your egg salad.

envelope sorter

Occupational Hazards

YOUR JOB CAN MAKE YOU SICK. Mentally. Or physically. Or both.

Naturally, Working Girl had such a job. Picture a
warehouse-size room filled with enormous noisy
machines—a factory, but not a factory making anything *useful*. No, it was a junk mail factory. Here the
correspondence you throw out without looking at was
printed, folded, addressed, stuffed, and mailed.

Working Girl's machine printed addresses on
envelopes. As the machine spat them out, her job

was to scoop them up, fan through them to check for blanks, and pack them into boxes.

That's it. Not only was the work stupefying, the conditions were inhumane. When all the machines were running, which was all the time, the noise was so deafening that if you wanted to talk to a co-worker you had to press your lips against her ear and holler. Even then she could barely hear you.[*]

By the end of an eight-hour shift, Working Girl had a pounding headache, her IQ had dropped 40 points, and who knows what permanent hearing damage was done. True, working in a slaughterhouse or coal mine would've been worse. But WG lasted only three weeks as an envelope sorter.

It's up to you to decide on the level of hazard you will put up with at work.

Some jobs are risky by definition. Firefighters know from the start their work is dangerous but they do it anyway, bless them.

Some jobs start off okay but become bad for you over time. Too many years at a computer can do a number on your wrists and neck, and force you to rethink the way you do your job.

Some jobs are unhealthy but don't need to be. Bad bosses, bullying co-workers, improper equipment, poor lighting, or insufficient ventilation can make you

---

[*] No, we didn't have ear protection. This was pre-OSHA. And yes, all the workers were women.

crazy and/or sick in short order.

While you may work at a risky or stressful or dangerous job voluntarily, most of the time we find ourselves in these positions because we didn't know what we were getting into or because a good job turned into a bad one.

Why do we stay? The money may be good, or we feel trapped, or we keep hoping things will improve. But no job is forever (see "Fear & Loathing," page 25) and in the long run you should not stay at a job that is bad for you. Something's gotta give.

Don't let that something be your health.

writer
for
hire

Do the Right Thing

COME, TAKE THE WALK OF SHAME WITH WORKING GIRL.

It happened late one night. Working Girl was on a high-stress, 20-hour-a-day proposal-writing assignment, part of a team of writers working directly for bigwigs flown in from the client's New York office.

The biggest bigwig was Greg, a smart, focused, destined-for-greatness guy in his mid-30's. Did Working Girl mention Greg was African-American? No? Well, he was, and it's important to the story.

From the start, Working Girl liked Greg and Greg liked Working Girl. It was one of those kindred-spirit things.

Each knew the other could be trusted and counted upon. You know how with some people you just immediately hit it off? That's how it was with WG and Greg.

Then came the night in question. It was, oh, 2 a.m.-ish. Working Girl was looking for Greg and finally found him in the lunchroom getting a cup of coffee.

"Oh, hi, there you are! I've been looking all over for you!" she said. "I don't mean to be a slave driver but we really need you in the conference roo——"

Um. Wait. That didn't sound good. But the words were out there. Oh no.

What did Working Girl do? Did she apologize for being a mindless idiot? Did she clear the air, making sure Greg understood she meant nothing—nothing!— by this horrible and stupid expression?

She did not. She ran out of the lunchroom and later pretended nothing had happened. Greg, to his eternal credit, continued to treat her as a friend, and they continued to work well together.

Mistakes. We offend a customer or colleague, we send a private email to the entire company address book, we miss a meeting, we break expensive equip-ment, we put our big fat feet in our big fat mouths. Everyone does the occasional stupid thing.

It's how you handle it that sets you apart from the crowd:

#1 Admit. Speak up immediately. Whatever you did or didn't do is going to be discovered anyway. Be the one with the courage to confess.

#2 Apologize. Show remorse. Take responsibility. People, especially bosses, hate a "whatever" attitude more than the original blunder.

#3 Analyze. Present a plan for fixing the mistake, if this is possible. Offer to do so on your own time. Learn from it.

Most important: Don't hide your mistake, deny it, make lame excuses, blame others, argue, or cry. Running out of the room is also a dumb move and just makes you look like a fool.

By now Greg has most likely forgotten the whole incident. Working Girl, however, still remembers it as if it were yesterday. Whenever she drives past the building where it happened, she cringes.

Greg, wherever you are, please know that Working Girl is really truly sorry.

ETERNAL TRUTH
A mistake stays a mistake only until you correct it.

Moonlighting

IN A WORLD LONG AGO AND FAR AWAY, Working Girl
moved from the sticks (Phoenix, AZ) to the big city
(Washington, D.C.). By week two, she'd landed her
first "real" job: secretary. Salary: $8,000 a year.
Double what she'd been earning as a store clerk in
Phoenix.

Hot dog.

So you're wondering, *How many weeks did it take
her to realize you can't live in Washington, D.C., on
$8,000 a year, even long ago and far away?* Not many!
After only a month, Working Girl was working a
second job.

Her schedule:

8-12: type

12-1: eat yogurt w/cut-up banana and raisins

1-5: type

5-6: eat bagel w/cream cheese, drink carton of milk

6-10: type

You no doubt spotted the problem right away. It took Working Girl a bit longer because, you see, she's always liked to type. She thought 12 hours a day at a keyboard wouldn't be bad. But it is bad. A typical evening shift: Hand-typing letters to members of Congress. You know what? After you have typed the same letter 535 times you want to cry.

Which brings us to the first rule of moonlighting:

Make your night job the opposite of your day job.

If you sit at a computer all day, get an evening gig where you'll be on your feet. If your real job is mentally taxing (software design), get a relatively easy second job (flower arranging). If at job #1 you deal with lots of people, seek solitude at job #2.

Here are five more things to remember about working multiple jobs:

- Be clear on which is your "real" job. Don't let #2 interfere with #1.

- Find a second job that is enjoyable to you, one you'll look forward to all day.
- Check if your company forbids or limits moonlighting. Some do.
- Don't get a night job with a competitor. (Duh.)
- Be upfront with both employers about your double worker status. Life is too short for lies and deception. Besides, working two jobs will be tiring enough.

Warning: Moonlighting can be addictive. You can take on a temporary second job to pay off your credit card or save for a vacation, and then discover that you like having the extra money so much you don't want to give it up. Every now and then, reassess your situation. Is what you're doing part of your overall life plan, or have you gotten sidetracked?

For the most part, though, moonlighting is empowering. Sure, it's stressful, and your social life suffers. But knowing that you are capable of working very hard for very long is knowing something important about yourself. It can make you feel wonderful. (Just don't get carried away.)

ETERNAL TRUTH

It's easier to work for money than it is to worry about not having enough money.

Jennifer H.S., OPHTHALMOLOGIST/PROFESSOR/
RESEARCH/LOBBYIST/CONSULTANT

"In addition to my professional roles, I'm married with two little boys. What keeps me sane is that I get eight hours of sleep. I go to bed right after the boys, read a novel for an hour, and then lights out. Sounds obvious, but sleep is almost unfashionable these days. People even brag about how little they sleep—like 'I get by on only four hours a night'—but this is BAD for you, and unproductive. Anyway, I think it's smarter to figure out what time of day you're most effective and do your work then."

The Boss From Hell

WORKING GIRL ONCE HAD A BOSS WHO called her in to the boardroom every couple weeks and said these words:

"You aren't very smart. You'll never find happiness. You will not succeed in this or any other job you might have in the future."[*]

That's a little weird. But what's weirder is that Working Girl stayed with this boss for two years.

Why? Well, she needed the work, jobs were scarce then, and she had an unemployed husband.

[*] Why did the BFH say this? The reason is simple. The BFH was crazy. Truly. Crazy people are everywhere, and occasionally they get promoted to positions of responsibility.

But even worse was that Working Girl half-feared the boss was right. She didn't know where her life was headed. She was barely making ends meet. She was stuck in an awful job. Maybe the Boss From Hell was right. Maybe she *wasn't* very smart.

Could this happen to you? No, because you are reading this book! So let's talk about what you need to do if you encounter your own Boss From Hell.

First, you need to know two things:

#1 You can't change a boss. (Or anyone. You can only change yourself.)

#2 In a direct power struggle with a boss, you will not win. (Sorry.)

Makes you want to up and quit right now, doesn't it? And that may be just what you do. But sometimes the work is something you're passionate about; other times you need the money and can't immediately find another job. Never fear. It is possible to handle a Boss From Hell. It takes nerve and it takes effort, but it can be done.

WG's 10 Tips for Handling the Boss From Hell

#1 Never show the stress is getting to you.

#2 Always behave in a way that earns respect.

#3 Find someone outside of work to confide in.

#4 Build strong ties with other managers and co-workers.

#5 Respond to the substance of the boss's criticism, not the tone.

#6 Study patterns. Is the boss freakiest right before lunch? Just after meetings? That's when to steer clear.

#7 Put everything in writing. When you receive verbal instructions, write an email summarizing them. Ditto for progress reports.

#8 Adopt an attitude of "joyful defiance." Do your work and love your work. It will help to keep you sane long enough to get to the next boss.

#9 If you decide to try addressing the problem, do it when the boss is in a good mood. Use a non-judgmental tone of voice. Start by saying, "What can I do to improve how we work together?"

#10 Your last resort is HR (if your company has HR). Describe what things you've tried to solve the problem. Be unemotional. Have documentation. Know what you're asking for—a transfer? A severance package? Know that HR works best when the boss's behavior is clearly illegal. And be prepared. They may walk you right out the door.

Fortunately, true Bosses From Hell are few and far between. Most bosses are nice people. In fact, most bosses are just muddling along as best they can. Maybe they got to be boss because they were good at something else and got promoted, they know how to play the power game, or they are related to an Upper Up. No one trained them in leadership, and they are freaked out.

> **ETERNAL TRUTH**
> It's as important to know how to manage your boss as it is to know how to do your job.

That's why every boss, whether naughty or nice, needs to be managed.

WG's 5 Tips for Managing Your Boss

#1 Keep the boss informed.

#2 Do things the way the boss wants them done.

#3 Accommodate the boss's communication style.

#4 Balance out the boss's weaknesses.

#5 Know the boss's hot buttons and avoid pushing them.

Do all these things and your boss will feel secure. Your boss's sense of security is directly related to your job happiness. Make 'em feel cozy and you will be rewarded. Maybe even with money.

envelope addresser

You're Fired

HEY, GUESS WHAT. You're gonna lose a job. Yup, chances are sooner or later you will be fired, let go, laid off, sacked, canned, terminated, dismissed, down-sized, rightsized, made redundant, or given the boot.

So when the boss says, "I'm sorry, we're letting you go because blah blah blah," what do you do?

- **Compose** yourself. Take a big deep breath in. Let a big deep breath out.

- **Compartmentalize** your fear, anger, and disbelief. Later you will vent and deal with them, in the company of loved ones.

- Claim your rights. Ask, "Is there severance pay? How much? What about my unused vacation and sick days? What reference do you plan to give for me? Do you offer any help getting a new job?" [*]

- Compliment your employer. No matter how awful a job was, you can always honestly say, "Thank you. I learned a lot working here."

- Clear out with class. Gather your stuff and leave on a positive note. Wish your boss and co-workers well—remember all these people are now part of your network (see "Weaving Your Web," page 87).

There's more. Here's what not to do:

- Do not be insulted if an "escort" stays with you while you pack up and leave. It's standard practice at many companies.

- Do not tell the boss he's a jerk. Even if he is.

- Do not plead to keep your job. It's too late. When you're let go, let go.

A lot of people lose their jobs. Try to learn from it. If you're canned for cause (tardiness, poor performance, bad attitude), take an honest look at yourself. You may be in the wrong job for you. You may have

---

[*] If you're being fired for poor performance, it doesn't hurt to ask, "May I resign instead?"

other problems. Now's your chance to fix them.

Sometimes a job loss has nothing to do with you or your work (see box). Your employer may not even tell you the truth about why you're getting booted. The fear of lawsuits looms large. Learn to figure things out for yourself, and remember, you are in charge of your own life and career.

SIGNS YOU'RE ABOUT TO BE LAID OFF

- Your workload is reduced.
- You start getting memos about the company's "new direction."
- Your company introduces technology that replaces humans.
- Your company closes branches in the name of "consolidation."
- Your company is sold to, or merges with, another company.
- Your industry is entering a recession.
- Your boss asks if you'd consider a pay decrease.
- Your boss is replaced by someone who's bringing in a hand-picked team.

Sometimes losing your job can be the best thing that ever happened to you. Want an example? Coming right up:

Working Girl once worked for a debt-collection agency typing addresses onto envelopes. It was a nasty place. The collectors treated the debtors like the scum of the earth (even though the debts were medical, like families owing $50,000 on little Johnny's leukemia). One of the collectors was a child molester (much later it came out that on weekends he used the office for his criminal activities). All the collectors chain-smoked (if Working Girl coughed or complained they told her, "You should start smoking too. Then it wouldn't bother you.")

Working Girl did a decent job, but she had reservations. She pitied the debtors. She would defend them to the collectors, but they just laughed at her. Then one day the boss called her aside and said, "Your attitude is bad for morale here. You just don't fit in. We're letting you go."

"Really?" said Working Girl. "Gosh. Thanks."

Getting fired. It happens to the nicest people.

JOB SURVIVAL TIP

Janice, BETWEEN JOBS

"I've been laid off eight times. Now I have a routine.
I go home and let myself cry for a while. Then I rewatch
Thelma and Louise. Then I exercise until I'm really
tired. Then I lie down on the floor and close my eyes
and remember a beautiful day when I was little when
we went to the beach. The world seemed wonderful
and full of possibilities on that day. I try to fill myself
up with that feeling. Then the very next day I start to
look for a new job."

CONFIDENT

Weaving Your Web

LOOKING FOR A JOB? Let's get this out of the way right now:

It *is* who you know.

Employers are human. Meaning, they prefer to minimize risk whenever possible. One way is to hire people whom they know or who know people they know.

So get to know some people.

A mini-example: Working Girl had an editing gig she adored, but the company went belly-up. Like dandelions, the principals scattered and started up their own little businesses. In the years since then, Working Girl has worked, freelance, for every single one of these companies.

That network practically created itself. But most of the time you build a professional network person by person, relationship by relationship. How?

You build a network by:
- taking classes and seminars
- showing up at trade shows and company functions
- attending lecture series and art exhibits
- joining civic groups and political parties
- volunteering to work for worthy causes
- going to professional association meetings, networking luncheons, class reunions, sporting events, conferences, parties, church, job fairs, and the gym
- using social networking sites, such as LinkedIn

That's not all. You can't just show up. You need to sincerely connect with the people you meet. You're not just collecting names for your database (yes, you should be keeping a database, on your trusty laptop, of everyone you know). You are forming real connections.

That means:

- showing true interest in people
- introducing them to others you think they might like
- sending them clippings you know would interest them
- remembering them with a note in their times of joy or sorrow
- donating to their causes
- referring business their way
- meeting for coffee
- being someone who's nice to know

Bottom line: You're not just collecting, you're connecting.

It ain't rocket science, but network-building does have rules. There are three:

#1 Renew the contact at least once a year (more is better). The annual end-of-the-year card is traditional, but you could be original and send a note on Flag Day or the vernal equinox. Creativity counts.

#2 Be equally nice to everyone, even "unimportant" people. It's the decent thing to do. They are often the gatekeepers to other people you need to meet, and you never know, you could walk in to work one day and find they are your next boss.

#3 Really listen to people when they talk.

The key to building a fabulous network is to give before you get. Some of your connections will turn into true friendships. How great is that? After all, relationships with other people are what life is all about. The fact that contacts are the best way to find a job is just a lovely, lovely fringe benefit! Be a good human being, and good things will come to you.

Oh, and don't forget to back up your database.

ETERNAL TRUTH
Make friends before you need them.

pollster

Can You
Hear Me Now?

DINNER'S READY!

You settle down at the table, spread your napkin
across your knees, pick up your fork, spear that first
luscious morsel of broccoli, raise it to your lips, and...

R-r-r-ring.

Phone calls at suppertime. Doncha just hate them?
It's probably someone selling fiberglass siding or a
new mortgage.

Or . . . it's Working Girl. Yep, WG once worked as a

telephone pollster. Did she interrupt you at dinner? She did? She must apologize. Please forgive her.

You may even find it in your heart to pity her, because cold-calling is no picnic. You put up with more rejection in an evening than most people do in a year. Bet you're thinking, *Boy, I'd never do a job like that!*

You know what? You, dear fellow working girl, no matter what career you decide to pursue, need to know how to cold-call.

Most jobs are not advertised. You find them through contacts (see "Weaving Your Web," page 87) and through research (see "Advanced Job Hunting," page 95). A super-effective way to find these "invisible" jobs is to cold-call. Don't worry—cold-calling can be learned. By anyone. Once you know how, you will be Unstoppable.

All you gotta do is write down what you're going to say and practice it until it is all of these things:

- Fast. State your name, what you have to offer, and what you want in 30 seconds. Rehearse out loud, in front of a mirror, until you are perfect.
- Friendly. Let your personality shine out. Stand up and smile while you speak—it gives your voice more energy. Always ask, "Is this a good time?"
- Focused. Being clear about what you want, in this case an interview, is the only way to get it.

Still nervous? Of course you are. Unless you're a born politician, cold-calling is always going to give you the willies. But remember! You are a worthy human being with something valuable to offer the company you're calling. You are trying to help them.

And here's a tip for younger working girls: Aim your calls toward senior executives. They are sometimes willing to help a young person and are at a place in their lives when they may want to mentor. Plus they won't be threatened by your assertiveness.

But, but, but . . . what if you cold-call and the person says, "Get lost, cupcake?" There is one sure thing about cold-calling: You will be rejected. You will probably be rejected 9 times out of 10. The only way to get to a Yes is to go through the Nos.

Everyone knows how difficult cold-calling is. Do a decent job of it and the person on the other end of the line will respect you for trying. Most people are nice, thank goodness. (Speaking of nice, never forget to thank people for their time.)

The best thing about cold-calling is that once you know how, the other elements of job hunting seem easy. So learn to give good phone. It will put you way ahead of the game.

Caroline, REALTOR

"It's hard to make cold calls because you're asking for something. So I pretend I'm Scarlett Johansson. I go all out, as if I'm trying for the Academy Award. If I succeed, I feel great. If I crash and burn, I tell myself it wasn't me they didn't like, it was Scarlett."

scientific editor

Advanced
Job Hunting

AFTER ONLY 51 JOBS, WORKING GIRL FOUND ONE SHE LOVED.

Get ready, because it's exciting. Are you sitting down? Take a deep breath. Okay, here goes: It's freelance scientific editing.

Yup. Scientific editing is work that Working Girl loves. She loves grammar, relishes learning new stuff, and delights in spotting other people's errors. Scientific editing involves collaborating with scientists, who are fun people (seriously). The freelance part is good, because it allows her time to do things like write this book. Throw in the fact that she feels like she's saving the planet (these are *environmental* scientists) and it's a home run, workwise.

You should have such a perfect a job. And you can. Here's all you have to do:

Step One: Get clear on what you want and what you have to offer.

Step Two: Find an employer who needs that.

Step Three: Put the two together.

Sound simplistic? Read the next sentence out loud because it's huge:

The best way to get a job you will LOVE is to figure out

- WHAT you want to do,
- WHERE you want to do it,
- and WHO you want to do it for,
- and then go apply at places that supply all that, whether or not they "have an opening."

With this method, you never have to bother with want ads, job boards, employment agencies, personnel, or human resources. At least not much.

HIRING YOUR BOSS

You can tell a lot about potential bosses at a first meeting. How do they talk and gesture, will they look you in the eye, what does their workspace look like, do they speak well of their employees?

You want a boss who will look out for you, who will teach you new things, and who will help you get to where you ultimately want to go.

You DO have to bother with networking (see "Weaving Your Web," page 87). Also cold-calling (see "Can You Hear Me Now?" page 91). Also, you need to have something of value to offer a prospective employer (see "The Right Stuff," page 180).

Advanced job hunting is a big project. You may spend years searching for, and landing, that perfect career. The first step is to identify your true calling (see "Take This Job and Love It," page 232). Once you think you've nailed that, it's time to start the hunt.

Here are a few tips:

- Be prepared. Create a one-minute statement of purpose. That's what you want to do (and why) and where you want to do it (and why). Memorize it. Say it to anyone who shows the least bit of interest.

- **Be cool.** Job hunt from a position of strength—while you still have a job. If that's not possible, have money saved up (enough to live on for at least three months). Do not allow yourself to get into a desperate situation. (Yes, WG knows, it's hard.) People can smell desperation a mile away, and they don't like it.

- **Be irresistible.** Build a website about what you can do and what you want to do. Write a blog about your area of interest. Post comments on other blogs.

- **Be in the loop.** Ask for help. Send your references your current résumé. Keep them up-to-date on what employers you're pursuing. Let them know what you'd like them to say when they're contacted.

- **Be thorough.** Find out as much as you can about potential employers. Troll the Internet, talk to current and former employees, read company publications, check to see what magazines and newspapers are saying about them.

- **Be persistent.** Once you've identified a place you want to work, do not give up if on your first approach you're told "nothing is available right now." Keep in touch, nicely. That person you interviewed is now part of your network.

- **Be real.** Arrogance is such a turnoff. Be rational and realistic about what you have to offer.

Oh, and be patient. Let's face it—you'll probably work at a few less-than-perfect jobs before you find The One.

Working Girl worked at 51 of 'em.

marketing writer

A Résumé Won't Get You a Job,
but You Need One Anyway

IT WAS THE CLASSIC SEEK JOB/GET JOB/LOSE JOB SCENARIO.

In Paris, Working Girl interviewed to write a sales brochure for the French branch of a British aviation company.

"Great," they said, eyeing the ten years' experience in aerospace writing on her résumé. "You're hired."

She researched, she drafted, she polished, and she delivered the text in three days. What a star! The French guys sent it off to the headquarters guys in England. Two days later it came back with this note: "Text written in U.S. English. We can't use."

But, but . . . of course it was written in "U.S. English." * Isn't Working Girl as American as apple pie? It was right there on her résumé: "Nationality: U.S."

The bad news: You can write the perfect résumé, but you can't make 'em read it.

More bad news: You have to write the perfect résumé anyway.

Even more bad news: If you think Working Girl is going to tell you step-by-step how to write your perfect résumé, think again, duckie.

Everyone's résumé is, or should be, different. It's unique to you, your background, and your dreams. And you will always be tweaking it. Fortunately, the amount of help out there—websites, career counselors, résumé-writing services, entire books—is amazing. Go and do what you gotta do. Devote time to working on your résumé. But not too much time! Don't obsess! If you spend more than two weeks, you have spent too long.

* Working Girl got paid anyway. Good old French guys!

A RÉSUMÉ IS . . .

- tailored to the job you're seeking
- a list of accomplishments, not duties
- accurate/honest
- appealing to look at
- easy to read

Never forget that a résumé is not a magic bullet. It will not get you a job. It may not even get you an interview. You need one, but it's not your only job-hunting tool.

In Working Girl's humble opinion, the best use of a résumé is as a "leave-behind." You give it to potential employers after the interview, which you got through your fabulous network. Once you've wowed them in person, your résumé stays behind as a reminder of your wonderfulness.[*]

Speaking of interviews, keep reading . . .

---

[*] However, many employers insist on seeing your résumé before they see you. So it's gotta be Perfect.

document
manager

The Interview

YOU'VE NETWORKED, YOU'VE COLD-CALLED, you've researched, you've résumé-ed, and you've finally snagged an interview for a job you really want.

Now all you have to do is convince the employer it would be a good idea to hire you.

Do you want to hear something surprising and a little bit disturbing?

Jobs don't go to the best candidates.

Jobs go to the candidates employers like best.

Therefore, your primary task at any interview is to *make the employer like you.*

How do you make someone like you, you ask.
There are ways, dear fellow working girl, there are
ways:

Way #1: Like them first.
It's human nature. We like people who like us. So at a
job interview, look for something to enjoy about the
interviewer. Is he/she funny, smart, shy, brisk? A person's main character traits show up within the first few
minutes of meeting. Find and focus on the nice ones.

Way #2: Don't scare them.
In a job interview, this means arriving on time
dressed in a way the employer is used to and showing by your behavior that you can do (or learn to do)
the job you're applying for. Employers are looking for
someone they feel will fit in, someone they wouldn't
mind spending eight or more hours a day with.

Way #3: Be engaged.
Nothing makes people happier than when someone
pays attention to them. So pay attention to your interviewer. Lean forward in your chair, establish good eye
contact, nod, ask questions the interviewer might enjoy
answering ("How did you get into this line of work?").
Be fully present. Show you are happy to be there.

Way #4: Radiate agreeability.
Assume goodwill on the part of others (don't be

offended if you're kept waiting for five minutes, for example), speak well of people (even your former horrible boss), act as if you are relaxed (you won't really be—fake it!). Smile, sit up straight. Rest your hands, palms up, in your lap. Keep your breathing even and soft.

SHOW, DON'T TELL

Bring a portfolio, a sample product, a letter of recommendation from a former boss or teacher, an award or certificate, a thank-you letter from a happy customer—something tangible that you can hand to the interviewer. People love show and tell.

Sometimes a thing as simple as showing that you can laugh at yourself clinches the deal. Here's what happened to Working Girl:

It was one of those interviews-by-a-panel-of-people. Working Girl had arrived on time, dressed to fit in, armed with answers to questions like, "What are your salary expectations?" She'd researched the company and decided here was a good place to work.

Things were going fine, and then one of the interviewers began to needle her.

"What if you changed someone's work and he

questioned it," he asked. "What if the person got offended? What if he argued? What if he got upset? What if he threw the document down on your desk, waved his arms, and screamed?"

What if, what if? Working Girl scrambled to respond to each question. But she ran out of answers before the interviewer ran out of hypothetical situations.

Finally she thought, "This is crazy. He's got to be kidding." So—she laughed. Not at the interviewer. At herself. At the situation.

Everyone in the room relaxed.

A year later her boss remarked, "I knew you would fit in here when you just laughed during those crazy interview questions."

BE ACTIVE, NOT PASSIVE

In general, the more you let an interviewer talk, the better (people love to hear themselves talk), but you still need to ask some smart questions:

- Is this a new position?
- If not, why is it open?
- Did the last person leave things in good shape?
- Do you foresee any changes for this position?
- Are there any existing problems I'd need to fix?
- What is your management style?
- What are the company's plans for growth?

JOB SURVIVAL TIP

Melissa, COMMUNICATIONS EXPERT

"When I interview, I mentally project fun positive thoughts. I send them the magic mojo! In my mind I think things like, 'You're a wonderful person. I am just the person you're looking for.' I believe that people respond to the energetic connection I'm creating, and that projecting these thoughts makes me come off as stronger and more positive."

paper
boy

Show Me
the Money

CONGRATULATIONS! You have reached the most powerful moment of your job hunt:

The moment after you've been offered a job and before you say yes.

Use this moment to negotiate your pay and perks.

"But I can't negotiate!" you might exclaim. It's a job that pays a set rate, say, or you are so desperate/ eager for work that you dare not rock the boat.

First, you can always negotiate *something*. And, second, negotiating pay is not "rocking the boat." It's being smart. People respect you for being smart.

Working Girl knows all this because she's suffered the consequences of failure to negotiate. Oh yeah.

The summer she was 10, she took on three paper routes for one of her brothers. For three months she pedaled her trusty blue Schwinn, named Speedy, all over Plainview, Minnesota, delivering the morning papers, the evening papers, and the big fat Sunday papers. In August she got paid.

"Here," her brother said, handing her $5.

"This is it?" said Working Girl.

He didn't have to answer because her other, older, brother butted in. "The time for negotiation is past," he intoned. "Did you establish a clear contract at the outset?"

Working Girl was not given a chance to answer.

"No, you did not," he continued. "Did you establish how much you would be paid before you took the job?" No. "Did you get anything in writing?" No again.

"In fact," he added, "you should be happy. You have just learned one of the most important laws of the marketplace: negotiate your pay."

Dear reader, don't do as Working Girl does. Do as she says.

Working Girl's 8 Laws
of Salary Negotiation:

#1 Know the going rate. Research salary.com and monster.com. Ask people in the field. Consult trade journals and professional groups. Go to the library.

#2 Decide on your Ideal Pay. It's the number you'd be proud to flaunt (not that you would).

#3 Decide on your Rock Bottom Price. It's the number right above the one you would despise yourself for accepting.

#4 Realize negotiation is a game and make up your mind to have fun playing it. The only rule: Do not be the first to name a number. (Because what if it's $20,000 less than what they would normally pay?) For example,

> Them: "Your qualifications are great. What salary are you looking for?"

> You: "I'm receptive to an offer. What's your range for this position?"

#5 Be pleasant, calm, honest. You may, however, need to be evasive. For example,

> Them: "What salary do you make now?"

> You: "My research shows that the market rate for someone with my skills and

experience is $XX. Does that coincide with your range?"

#6 Don't accept immediately. Thank them and ask for a day to think about it.

#7 Spend this day crunching numbers. Don't forget perks. Bonuses, an extra vacation day, decent insurance, a car, etc., can make up for a low-ish salary.

#8 *Important:* Have a Plan B. Before you talk money, prepare a doable and attractive (to you) plan of action for what you'd do if you don't get the job. A viable alternative in your mind will make you calm. Also, irresistible.

Finally, if after thinking and crunching you decide to take the job, ask for the offer to be put in a letter that spells out both your responsibilities and your compensation. If this practice is not standard for the job you're getting, at least try to get the offer via email. Didn't your brothers tell you to always get things in writing?

Well, if they didn't, Working Girl is telling you now.

ETERNAL TRUTH

If you don't ask for something, you will never get it.

freelance journalist

How to Work

KNOWING HOW TO DO YOUR JOB (writing code, teaching French, brewing lattes, cutting hair, building websites, filling teeth) is important.

But knowing *how to work* is even more important.

Good how-to-work skills are essential. They're the key to being a productive, efficient, relaxed, and happy working girl all your life long.

How-to-work skills are universal—you carry them with you from job to job.

How-to-work skills can make the difference between career success and career . . . failure.

Employers adore a person with good how-to-work skills.

In fact—and get ready because this may sound a little weird—the most important thing Working Girl learned from having 59 jobs is that how you do your work is as important as what results you achieve.

If you have terrible work habits and are an incredible pain to work with, people aren't going to want you around no matter how great your finished product is. Sometimes, superior how-to-work skills can even get you a promotion that you're not otherwise qualified for. And, of course, knowing how to work is what keeps you in your job.

Also true, and equally weird, is that many employers will assume you already know how to work. If you don't, they are surprised or upset or worse. Why is something so important so rarely spelled out? Who knows.

With no further ado, here are Working Girl's Twelve Commandments of How to Work. All learned by trial and error, of course.

the 12 Commandments
of How to Work

1. Do even the non-fun parts of a job with class.

2. Agree only to commitments you know you can meet.

3. Learn to predict how long it takes you to do stuff.

4. Anticipate things will go wrong. Have a Plan B. Maybe even C.

5. When others are freaking out, do not join them.

6. Treat everyone at work equally well.

7. Everything you do/say/email should make you look smart. Or at least rational.

8. Listen to people; act as if you care.

9. Be slow to take offense.

10. Don't tell your boss anything you wouldn't tell a total stranger.

11. Take the time to be careful; make the effort to be accurate.

12. Carry projects all the way through to their logical conclusions.

You may be saying to yourself, *These command-ments are pretty easy.*

But what is not easy is to do All Twelve Commandments All The Time. Come to think of it—consistency, that's another great how-to-work skill!

Knowing how to work has another very cool benefit. It makes you good to be around. Your co-workers will think you are amazing. Your boss will respect and value and promote you. Your clients, if you are free-lance, will hire and rehire you.

One of Working Girl's favorite recurring jobs in Paris kept coming back and back simply because she was always able to meet the deadline (Commandment #2). Here's how it went:

R-r-r-ing.

"Hello?" said Working Girl.

"Hey. Davidson here. I need 1,500 words for the January issue."

"Sounds good."

"The thing is, I need it by Friday. Can you do it?"

"Let me check my calendar. How many people would I need to interview?"

"Three."

"Are they local?"

"Yes."

"Do you need photos?"

"We'll use stock."

"Yes, I can do it."

This magazine rarely hired freelancers. But when the editor needed last-minute filler, he knew he could call on Working Girl. She loved it. Only three days of intense work and bingo, payday. It was easy and fast money (and WG always needed money).

So go back and read those Commandments one more time. What the heck—two more times.

ETERNAL TRUTH

How you actually do your work is as important as the actual work you do.

JOB SURVIVAL TIP

Judy, MASSAGE THERAPIST

"Even if you love your job it doesn't mean you are as skilled or enthusiastic with every single part of it. I'm not crazy about bookkeeping, for example. So when it comes time to bringing the books up-to-date, I will 'set the stage.' I make sure I'm fed, exercised, rested. I tidy my office so everything is clean and organized. Taking care of myself and my physical space first helps me clear my mind and enables me to do a better and more efficient and faster job."

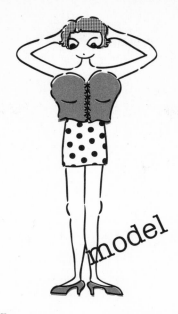

model

What to Wear, or Not

"*MADEMOISELLE*, YOU DO NOT HAVE A BEAUTIFUL BOSOM."

Working Girl once had a four-day job as a model at the Salon de Prêt à Porter, the famous fashion show held every year in Paris.

Yes, modeling. In Paris.

Of course, there was a catch. Her employer designed clothing for overweight women. Working Girl was a skinny thing back then (she only got the job because a friend of a friend of a friend knew this employer) and she did little for the muu-muus and housedresses she was expected to promote.

As a last resort, the employer made her try on a black lace bustier. Sexy underwear for overweight French housewives—who knew?

Working Girl stepped out of the dressing closet.

"*Mon Dieu,*" said the employer. She peered down into the bustier, where Working Girl's boobs looked lonely and a bit sad in the yawning pits of black lace.

"*Mademoiselle!*" the employer exclaimed. Then, as if she did this every day, she plunged her hands down into the bustier, brought Working Girl's boobs up to the surface, and . . . fluffed them.

They swelled attractively for a moment before settling back down. Then the fateful words were spoken: "*Mademoiselle*, you do not have a beautiful bosom."

For the rest of the show, Working Girl unpacked boxes and fetched Camembert sandwiches for lunch. But she kept her eyes open and learned these three things:

· Clothes are never just clothes.

· Clothes are advertisements for a product.

· That product is *you*.

NOT BRAND X

Branding yourself is easy and doesn't have to be cheesy.

Just consistently wear a particular color or piece of jewelry or item of clothing and, voilà, you've created a signature look!

Whatever you choose, it should be something you love and that reflects you.

You can even take your "flaws" and turn them into advantages. If you have to wear glasses, for example, wear memorable glasses that look great on you. If your feet require that you wear orthotics, become known for your fabulous, funky, flat shoes.

Look around, and these are some of the sample ads you will see:

"I am powerful."

"I am smart."

"I am clueless."

"I am without any self-respect whatsoever."

"I am rich (or not rich!)."

"I do not own a full-length mirror."

Yup, your clothes send a message.

So use them to send a message that *helps* you.

Working Girl has only one simple guideline:

Wear what makes you feel strong.

What's that, you say?

Answer: You feel strong when your clothes are attractive, appropriate, and comfortable.

Okay, right, you're thinking, *How elementary. I already know this.* Of course you do. But a lot of the outfits Working Girl sees at work need work! So for those (not you) who do need help putting it all together, here are a few basic tips:

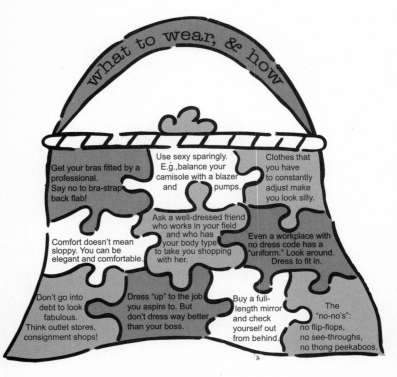

what to wear, & how

Get your bras fitted by a professional. Say no to bra-strap back flab!

Use sexy sparingly. E.g.,balance your camisole with a blazer and   pumps.

Clothes that you have to constantly adjust make you look silly.

Ask a well-dressed friend who works in your field and who has your body type to take you shopping with her.

Comfort doesn't mean sloppy. You can be elegant and comfortable.

Even a workplace with no dress code has a "uniform." Look around. Dress to fit in.

Don't go into debt to look fabulous. Think outlet stores, consignment shops!

Dress "up" to the job you aspire to. But don't dress way better than your boss.

Buy a full-length mirror and check yourself out from behind.

The "no-no's": no flip-flops, no see-throughs, no thong peekaboos.

Anne, PHOTOGRAPHER

"I specialize in black-and-white photography. My 'signature look' is to wear a black shoe with a white sock on one foot and a white shoe with a black sock on the other foot. I'm an artist, so I get away with it. It's fun and no one ever forgets me."

night
manager

Job Hopping

BY THE TIME WORKING GIRL WAS UP TO JOB
NUMBER 12 or so, people began to look at her funny.

A rolling stone gathers no moss, family/teachers/
friends reminded her.

Huh? *What would I do with moss?* she thought and
stuck to her standard operating procedure: If she
found a new job that paid more than her current job,
hippety-hop, off she went.

Then she resigned from a position she loved and
was good at (assistant manager at a House of Fabrics)
to take a new position (night manager at the competi-

tion, another fabric store down the street) for a nickel more an hour. Five cents. Whoop-de-do. The downside: whereas House of Fabrics had beautiful yard goods that were a pleasure to work with and the people who ran it loved sewing and fashion, "Store X" was a sad place full of sad people selling sad seconds.

Working Girl lasted only three months at Store X.

In your own career you will be, if not as much of a bunny rabbit as Working Girl, someone who changes jobs from time to time. It's the way things are now. There are even rules (turn page!).

ON YOUR FIRST WEEK AT A NEW JOB

· remember: You're the New Girl again

· be on time (better—be early)

· listen more than you talk

· ask intelligent questions

· always carry pen & paper so you can take notes

· steer clear of the grumblers

The 5 Rules of Job-Hopping

#1 Your job changes should look like part of a plan. Avoid random hopping.

#2 Why you hop is more important than how often. Best reason to hop: You want to learn new skills so you can be better at what you do.

#3 Pre-hop, always ask yourself: Am I running toward something or away from something?

#4 Hop gently. Do it without alienating people or leaving them in the lurch.

#5 Avoid the premature hop. Give a job a chance! Try to stay at least a year. Consider whether an internal move at your existing company is a better option.

Here is what Working Girl wants you to know about job-hopping: You should always be ready to hop. Not that you want to, or plan to, or have to. But you should always be ready. The only constant in your career is you. You should never allow yourself to become wholly dependent on any one employer. Your job could be outsourced, downsized, or made redundant in the twinkling of an eye.

So keep your skills and certifications and résumé

current, know the market pay rate for your job, maintain a wide acquaintance, have money in the bank, and cultivate the attitude that a new job is an exciting wonderful challenge!

Happy hopping.

JOB SURVIVAL TIP

Jennifer S., BANKER

"For my first week at any new job I prepare a 60-second speech on what I'm good at and what I want to learn. I say it, using the same words each time, to everyone I meet. It kind of 'brands' me. Plus I really think it's important to control your image, to control how people see you, and this is how I do it."

store assistant

Fried

"HEY YOU. TAKE THIS UP TO WHATSHERNAME AND TELL HER TO PUT IT OUT FRONT."

The manager kicked a sagging cardboard box and turned away. What he meant was, "Drag this refrigerator-size carton of fabric scraps up to Evelyn and ask her to add it to the end-of-month sale goods."

A boss who won't learn anyone's name. Co-workers too demoralized to object.

It was Working Girl's third fabric store job. With each store she'd slipped farther down the retail ladder until she'd landed here, at rock bottom.[*] She didn't know where this store got its merchandise and she didn't want to know. She'd started out in fabric sales as a lover of velvet and seersucker and crisp cotton duck. This stuff was bottom of the line, torn, stained—not seconds, not even thirds.

Job burnout. You will know it when you have it. Burnout is when the work to which you give your time and energy and maybe even love turns out to be unrewarding. You feel cheated, betrayed, used, broken. Burnout isn't the same as stress, which fills you with anxiety. Burnout does the opposite. It empties you, leaving only apathy. You're dried up, you're exhausted, and you just don't care anymore.

JOB BURNOUT—THE SYMPTOMS

Disappointment

Disillusionment

Detachment

Dullness

Despondence

Depression

Despair

---

[*] Working Girl had just moved cross-country. Desperate to start bringing in money, she took a terrible job. Try to avoid this!

Job burnout has two causes:

You are under too much job stress for too long.
For a while we can deal with long hours, low pay, con-
flicting demands, confusing instructions, harassment,
and lack of recognition. Burnout happens when we
let it go on and on, never seizing control of our lives.
Look for these signs: Exhaustion (even first thing in
the morning), cynicism (you do the bare minimum to
get by), and worthlessness (you feel you are a failure).

You are in the wrong job for you. When we try
to cram ourselves into jobs that don't suit us—
emotionally, mentally, spiritually, physically—we
sooner or later reach a breaking point. If this happens
to you, don't beat yourself up. Anyone can choose or
fall into or be pushed into a career that seemed like a
good idea at the time. At first you may even succeed
(because, let's face it, you can be good at many
things). But in the long run it will eat you alive.

The cure to job burnout is to discover what work
you were meant to do and then do it in a way that
suits your personality and life. Hey, isn't that the
point of this whole darn book?

Meanwhile, back at the ragbag fabric store.

"Miss, will this cotton chintz shrink?" asked a grandma in a homemade housedress.

Of course it will shrink. Where does she think she is?

"Well, if it were me—" Working Girl looked around. Her manager was right behind her. She took a big, deep breath. "Yes, ma'am, this fabric will certainly shrink. And possibly pill. The colors will run, too. And that thread you're buying—it will tangle in your bobbin and maybe ruin your machine and the first time you wash that dress it will pucker at the seams. These materials are not worth your time."

"Hey you!" shouted the boss.

Which brings us to the next chapter, "Quitting with Class," page 130.

ETERNAL TRUTH

Just because you can do a job doesn't mean you want to do—or should do—that job.

teller

Quitting with Class

NOTHING IS MORE FUN THAN QUITTING A JOB. Your task is to make it look as if it's not.

Why? Because when you resign, you reject. People don't like to be rejected. It's insulting and, in the case of your boss, inconvenient and expensive.

So when you quit a job—and you will—quit with class. Sure, that whoosh of freedom you get when you walk out the door for the last time feels great, but it will feel even greater knowing you've done everything right.

How to Be a (Fabulous) Quitter

STEP 1: BEFORE YOU GIVE NOTICE

- get your work up to date
- take all personal stuff off the company computer
- organize your work in a way others can understand
- check company guidelines for giving notice (if there aren't any, two weeks is standard)
- find out if you have benefits coming (unused vacation, comp time, etc.)

STEP 2: WHEN YOU GIVE NOTICE

- tell your boss first, in private, in person
- display regret, even if you're overjoyed (you're leaving— be kind)
- offer to train your replacement
- be prepared for your boss to say, "Why don't we make this your last day and we'll give you two weeks' salary as severance?" (some bosses take rejection personally—this is the reason for Step 1)

STEP 3: AFTER YOU GIVE NOTICE

- follow up with a letter of resignation, stating you are resigning as of such-and-such date (also, try to say something positive—e.g., how much you enjoyed working there—or if you didn't, how much you learned)
- do not brag to co-workers about your great new job (it's tacky)
- ask for a letter of recommendation, even if you already have a new job
- continue to do your job well, up to the last day, the last hour

After Step 3, remind yourself: When you quit a job, your boss and co-workers—immediately—cease to be boss and co-workers and become part of your network. Treat them with loving care (see "Weaving Your Web," page 87). Someday you might need them, because you are *always* looking for a job (see "Job Hopping," page 122). That's why you ask for a letter of recommendation from every boss. You are building up a nice little portfolio.

Now for a bit of truth telling.

Despite Working Girl's 59 jobs, she has received only one letter of recommendation in her entire career. And that one came without her asking for it. She didn't have this book, so she didn't know enough to ask for one!

The letter came from her manager at her bank teller job. It was warm and full of praise. It told a tale of a day the manager was late and Working Girl, who showed up first, took charge, got the branch ready for the day's business, and opened up on time. It made Working Girl look like a hero.

"Wow, thanks," said Working Girl to her soon-to-be-former boss. She didn't know what else to say. Especially since she had no memory of this incident. In fact, the incident *couldn't* have happened, because she didn't have a key to the bank. Was the manager confusing her with someone else? Was this the standard letter he gave everybody?

You wanna know what? Working Girl never asked. Why argue with a happy boss?

Out of Your
Comfort Zone

"HA HA HA HA!"

Working Girl looked around. What was so funny? Why did the audience explode with laughter every time the American character, a girl who always wore a fanny pack around her waist, uttered the words "my fanny pack"?

The play was brilliant, and it was lovely of her Irish co-workers to take her to the theater, but the fanny pack hilarity was just one of many mysteries Working

Girl encountered during her two-week stint writing manufacturing procedures for a foundry in Waterford, Ireland.

Her biggest problem was the language barrier. Yes, they do speak English in Ireland, but Working Girl suspected that her colleagues were buttering on the brogue extra thick for her benefit. Not out of cruelty. They were just, as they said, havin' a bit o' fun.

So as her group left the theater and headed for the pub next door, she wasn't shy about asking, "Why did everybody laugh every time the American character in the play said 'my fanny pack'?"

The men in the group snickered. The women sighed and shook their heads. No one wanted to explain.

"You see," one of them finally began, "in Ireland the—" She lowered her voice. "The 'fanny'—it's what we call, um—." Seconds passed. "It's what we call ... the place on the woman where the baby pops out!"

Oh.

It's a small, small, small, small world.* Have you noticed? More and more work is being done by international teams. Cultural diversity is not just a buzzword, it's a phenomenon. Everyone, including you, needs to learn how to function in unfamiliar situations.

---

* Shameless rip-off of 1963 film, It's a *Mad Mad Mad Mad World*.

The key is to get comfortable with confusion. Fortunately, it's sorta fun. Some tips:

Ask for help. When confusion strikes, say, "I don't understand. Please explain."

Adapt to others. Even within the same country, cultures vary from workplace to workplace. Be open to new ways of doing things.

Adjust your thinking. Explore your prejudices, habits, and expectations. They tell you a lot about yourself.

Accept that everything changes. Change is going to come anyway. Embracing it takes much less energy than fighting it.

ETERNAL TRUTH
The farther out of your comfort zone you leap, the more people will step forward to catch you.

Ambiguity is tiring. You will have bad days. When it all seems like too much, get yourself some quiet time. Reflect, relax, listen to some music, chat with your mom—whatever recharges your batteries. Learning how to function in unfamiliar situations, when you're not exactly sure what's what, is worth it because if you do it well you will never be caught off balance. You will be ready when new opportunities pop up. You will really be living.

Remember: It's the adventurous, open-minded ones who think the thoughts no one else has ever thought before. They are the ones who make the big discoveries, enjoy the most success, and have the most fun.

junior PR writer

Going Up?

MEMO

TO: Working Girl

FROM: Big Boss

RE: Promotion

Effective immediately, you will be promoted
to the position of junior public relations writer.

HOT DIGGETY DOG.

After seven years in clerical, Working Girl had finally wrapped her fingers around the very lowest rung of the middle management ladder.

"And, guess what, Betty!" she exclaimed. "I'm even getting my own private office!"

Betty, secretary to the Big Boss, licked a stamp and positioned it on the corner of an envelope. She didn't look up.

"It's right across from your desk," Working Girl continued. "I'll be able to see you, but I won't be sitting out here in the hall with you anymore. Will ya miss me?"

Betty set her lips in a straight line. She grabbed the envelope, rose, circled her desk—which stood out in the hallway like all the other secretaries' desks—and walked away.

What was wrong with *her*? Shouldn't she have been happy for Working Girl? It wasn't as if Betty had been gunning for the job. She was, like, sixty. A lifelong secretary.

Wanna lose friends fast? Get promoted above them. And then brag about it.

You may believe "nothing will change" when you get kicked upstairs. Your friends are your friends, right? And there are the rare exceptions. But, in general, once you're in a supervisory position, you are automatically no longer part of the gang. It's lonely at the top.

So, after the celebratory champagne/sparkling cider/latte/hot chocolate, brace yourself for these potential reactions from your former peers:

Resistance. It can be hard for people who still remember that holiday party where you stood on the copy machine and lip-synched to the Spice Girls to suddenly see you as a leader. They knew you when.

Suspicion. Of course, your promotion was awarded for your skill and performance. So you will be surprised to learn that some people conclude it was luck, politics, or favoritism. Or worse, that you slept with the boss.

Envy. A weird quirk of human nature is that people often resent success. Even colleagues who are happy for you may also, deep down, hate you a little. Whether or not they wanted the job themselves.

Isolation. Work friendships feel real. After all, you see these people every day, all day. But work friends are seldom really truly friends. Proof: When a job ends, the job friendships usually do, too (see "Friends," page 196).

So take things slowly. Assert your new authority gradually and gracefully. Ask for input. Be scrupulously fair. Use your power, such as it is, wisely. Keep in mind you will need to demonstrate, to those above and below you, why you got this promotion in the first place.

And Betty? Betty not only stopped being Working Girl's friend, she refused to answer her phone or open her mail. Even the Big Boss stepped in and tried to resolve the issue. But real life doesn't always come with a happy ending.

In the end Working Girl decided to just leave her be. Hope you're okay, Betty.

bus
boy

Do No Evil

IT WAS WORKING GIRL'S FIRST SHIFT AT HER NEW
BUSBOY JOB.

"Hey, what are you doing with that bread basket?"
barked her boss, owner and manager of the restaurant, a strip mall Italian joint.

Working Girl had been about to dump the contents
of the basket into the food waste barrel. "I just
bused these," she said.

"Those bread rolls are perfectly good! Add them to
another basket."

"Really? They're leftovers."

"I can't afford the waste."

"Oh."

"And another thing when you're busing. Napkins. If they don't look used, just refold them and set them out again."

"But aren't they . . . dirty?"

"Are you questioning me?"

"Ummm."

"Better not. I gotta make a living here!"

And that's how it usually looks when you are asked to do something unethical, immoral, illegal, or just plain icky at work. It looks like: No big deal, this is how it is in business, we need to stay competitive, everybody else is doing it, and grow up, girl, don't be so naïve.

In fact, sometimes it's hard to tell if a thing is unethical or not. All you may have to go on is a funny feeling in your stomach. Pay attention to funny feelings! Ask:

- If someone did this to me, how would I feel?

- Would I be proud to tell my grandmother about this?

- How would I feel about this in 10 years?

Other times it's obvious a thing is wrong. ("Just date these invoices for last month." "That old lead-based paint? Just pour it down the drain.")

Either way, it can be sticky. People never like to be told they're doing wrong. Especially when they're doing wrong. We don't expect our bosses to ask us to be dishonest. But it happens, in little and big ways, so it's good to think through in advance how you would react if it happens to you.

Here are five strategies that have worked for Working Girl:

#1 Just say no. Smile. Look your boss in the eye. Let a few seconds pass and then calmly say, "Well, you know, I'm just not comfortable doing that." This works more than half the time. Really.

#2 Rephrase the request. "You actually want me to tell the customer we're almost done with his order when we haven't even started?" Hearing how bad it sounds may cause your boss to reconsider.

#3 Suggest an alternative. "Why don't we just give people one dinner roll to start and offer them more if they want?" Most of the time it's results your boss cares about, not how you get those results.

#4 Be a hero. "I'm concerned this idea will hurt us/you/our company in the long run." Show how the dishonesty will harm your boss's interests; instantly become the company's most valued employee.

#5 Deflect with humor. "You want me to do *what*?!" Or, "Whoa, man, let's not go there." This works only if you are on very good terms with your boss and you are a natural-born comedian.

Oh, and the Italian restaurant job? Working Girl lasted a week. That's strategy number six: find a new and better employer.

> **ETERNAL TRUTH**
> If you refuse to tell the little lies, no one will ask you to tell a big lie.

newsletter editor

Fake It till You Make It

AFTER SIX MONTHS AS A JUNIOR PR WRITER, Working Girl was offered a promotion.

"Do you think you could write a weekly newsletter?" asked the Big Boss.

Working Girl liked to write. "Newsletter editor" sounded like a cool title. And the pay was $3,000 a year more than what she was currently earning.

"Sure," she said.

"It has to come out every Monday morning, no exceptions," said the BB.

"Okay."

"You'll have to generate all the story ideas on your own."

"No problem."

"You'll be interviewing mechanics down on the factory floor. All men. Will you mind?"

"Of course not."

"Your topic will be gas turbine engines. Quality and reliability stuff." The BB leaned back in his chair and yawned. "Do you think you can do it?"

Working Girl hesitated. Quality and reliability? What's that? Still. An extra $3K would come in awfully handy. She took a deep breath.

"Yes. I can do it."

The next day she went to the factory floor to interview her first mechanic. As Working Girl marched past in her navy blue dress-for-success suit and matching high heels, clutching her leatherette briefcase, every guy in the building froze. Every single one, his wrench or whatever hanging slack in his hands, stood with his mouth open, staring. You'd have thought they'd all been in jail for 30 years and not seen a woman the entire time.

Fear. You will feel it from time to time. Even if you don't have men gawking at you, a new job can be terrifying and can make you feel like, "I can't do it." But this is important: Don't show your fear. You can feel inadequate, vulnerable, greener than grass, scared witless, or totally unsure of yourself. It's okay to feel it. Just don't show it.

This is not wrong. This is not dishonest. This is the way you jump into the pool and learn to swim. Here are a few tips to get you dog-paddling:

FIVE TIPS FOR FAKING IT

1. Teach yourself to look relaxed. If someone asks, "How's it going?" smile and say, "Great."

2. Dress the part. It will give you a boost.

3. Accept that you'll make mistakes. Learn from them. Move on.

4. Keep your sense of humor.

5. Ask questions. You don't have to pretend you know everything. Remember, you are not faking competence, you are faking confidence.

Working Girl wrote and published that quality and reliability newsletter every blessed week for four years. She never missed a deadline.

And the factory floor mechanics? They continued to ogle her each time she came down to talk with them, and each time it was as if they hadn't seen a woman in 30 years.

burger girl

Perverts at Work

SPEAKING OF MEN, Working Girl has been propositioned, stalked, harassed, leered at, and wolf-whistled at by male co-workers, but only once was she physically attacked.

Not a bad record, really. Here's what happened:

Scene: Burger joint

Cast: Working Girl, 16, at front counter
　　　Don, 40ish, at grill

Day 1: "Sweet sixteen, never been kissed," said Don. Working Girl was 16, had indeed been kissed, but didn't see how it was any business of Don's. She kept her nose in the air.

Day 2: "Sweet sixteen, never been kissed," said Don. Working Girl pretended not to notice.

Days 3 through 68: "Sweet sixteen, never been kissed," said Don. Working Girl gritted her teeth.

LAST DAY ON THE JOB: Working Girl left without saying good-bye. But—oh no. Don followed her out to the parking lot.

She sprinted across the asphalt. She hopped into her car. She jammed her key into the ignition.

Too late.

"Sweet sixteen, never been kissed!" whispered Don as he reached through the open car window, grabbed Working Girl's shoulders, twisted her around, and kissed her long and hard right smack on the mouth.

He came up for air, licked his lips, and moved in for round two. But Working Girl started her car! She crammed it into drive! She peeled out of the parking lot! To this day she prays she ran over Don's foot on the way out.

Meanwhile, she has made this chart for you.

How to Deal

*No matter where you work, a man who thinks he
is God's gift to women will work there, too.*
Here are your (not 100% serious) options.

OPTION Dress frumpily.

UPSIDE You will save money on clothes.

DOWNSIDE You will hate yourself. Worse, even if the
original guy loses interest, you will find that you now
attract a lower class of weirdo.

OPTION Play dumb.

UPSIDE He concludes you are too innocent/stupid to
trifle with, and he stops.

DOWNSIDE He concludes he has found in you a soul
mate (i.e., someone as clueless as he is).

OPTION Avoid him.

UPSIDE Offers immediate short-term relief.

DOWNSIDE Often only a temporary fix. Is wimpy.

OPTION Ignore him.

UPSIDE Also offers immediate short-term relief.

DOWNSIDE Also often only temporary. Worse, he may
(a) decide you are "a challenge" or (b) find another
victim.

OPTION Yell at him.

UPSIDE Scared you will report him to the sexual harassment police, he stops.

DOWNSIDE The kind of man who in this day and age doesn't know sexual harassment can get him in trouble is the kind of man who will think your anger is cute.

OPTION Punch him in nose.

UPSIDE Effectively speaks to him in his own language— i.e., aggression.

DOWNSIDE Unless you are Xena, Warrior Princess, this option could backfire.

OPTION Make his life a living hell (sabotage his work, get him fired).

UPSIDE It could be fun.

DOWNSIDE It lowers you to his level.

OPTION Quit.

UPSIDE A quick and permanent solution. (Unless he proceeds to stalk you. But then he will no longer be a Pervert at Work, putting your situation outside the purview of this chart.)

DOWNSIDE You no longer have a job.

OPTION Laugh in his face.

UPSIDE Immensely satisfying for you, and a nice little power move.

DOWNSIDE He mistakes your scorn for delight.

OPTION Get yourself promoted above him.

UPSIDE Even more immensely satisfying.

DOWNSIDE May take a long time.

OPTION Report him to HR.

UPSIDE It makes the whole thing someone else's problem.

DOWNSIDE HR? Are you kidding?

OPTION Ask him, reasonably and maturely, to stop.

UPSIDE It's the reality check he needs, so it may work.

DOWNSIDE A guy like this checked out of reality so long ago it may be a waste of breath.

· ·

Does this sound as if there is no one good option? That's because there is no *one* good option.

Each sexual harassment case is unique. And, of course, it depends on the scale of the attack. There's a big difference between telling an off-color joke and demanding sex in return for keeping your job.

But in most cases, Working Girl recommends first trying to deal with the situation yourself. It's good practice (sadly, sexual harassment will always be with us). And you know what? Nine times out of ten, you'll be able to fix the problem on your own.

So play with the options (the serious ones). Try them alone, or in combo. But remember to keep good notes! Because if the guy continues to hassle you, you're going to report the jerk. Calmly. Rationally. Effectively.

P.S. Working Girl found that for her the most effective option was "Laugh in his face."

JOB SURVIVAL TIP

Trish, GRAPHIC ARTIST

"I work in an office with all men. It gets a little like *Animal House* in there some days! So I put a jar on my desk and labeled it, JAR OF SHAME. Whenever one of them says something offensive or crude, I make them put a dollar in the jar. It keeps them in line, and it pays for my lattes."

secretary

Who's the Boss

ONCE UPON A TIME WHEN WORKING GIRL WAS VERY
young, she moved to the big city and got a job as a
secretary.

She had no winter coat. She had only one pair of
shoes—sandals she wore even when it snowed. She
had exactly five outfits, one for each day of the work-
week. She had bad hair seven days a week and was
a stranger to mascara.

People were kind but patronizing. They would say,
"Young lady, do you think you would be able to
alphabetize magazines?" That sort of thing.

Then one day—it was October 31st—Working Girl was given an important assignment. She was to hire and supervise a temp, someone to hand-type fifty letters going to members of Congress and needing to look like personal correspondence. No computers back then! Normally Working Girl would have typed the fifty letters herself, but she had important other things to type that day.

The temp wore a sleek black wool suit and shiny black patent leather pumps. Working Girl was wearing one of her five outfits—a white blouse and a flowered cotton/polyester skirt she'd sewn herself. And the sandals.

"Here is the letterhead," Working Girl said to the temp. "Here is the letter you'll type. Be sure to date them all for tomorrow because that's when they need to go out."

The temp began to type. She typed all day long. Working Girl never interrupted her or scrutinized her work. She looked so sure of herself. Besides, Working Girl knew how irritating it was to have someone looking over your shoulder or treating you as if you were a nitwit.

At the end of the day, the temp went home, leaving a neat stack of fifty hand-typed letters.

The text was centered on the page.

White-Out/lift-off tape/strikeovers had not been used.

All words were correctly spelled.

But—you knew there would be a "but," didn't you?—every single blessed letter was dated:

October 32nd

Moral of the story: When or if it comes your turn to "be the boss," don't be shy about managing people. Use your power wisely (!), but use it. For tips on how, see "Going Up," page 138, and "Large and In Charge," the next chapter.

disciplinarian

Large and
in Charge

WORKING GIRL HOISTED THE FAT French-English
dictionary high over her head and let it fall to the
floor. The room went silent.

"Thank you," she said, enunciating clearly. "I am
tired of shouting at you to get your attention. If you
are not interested in learning English, fine. I do not
care if you ever learn English. I do not care if you all
lose your jobs. I would be happy to leave right now
and let you sit and chat in French all week long."

The students—French engineers in their forties—

shifted in their chairs and glanced at each other. From the moment they arrived for this weeklong English immersion course, they'd behaved like rowdy 10-year-olds. Cracking jokes, refusing to do the exercises, making faces. Not just in Working Girl's class, in all of them.

"What do you think? Do you want to learn English?" The school was in an old French convent and the classroom was cold but Working Girl could feel sweat beading up on her forehead.

"Y-yes," one man finally said. "Continue, please." The others nodded. And as if by magic, the naughty French schoolboys transformed into grown men and buckled down to their lessons.

Your lesson: You can be put in a position of power, but that doesn't automatically mean you'll be able to assert that power.

You need *authority*.

Authority comes from the belief that it is okay for you to instruct, direct, and correct people.

When you're young or inexperienced, you don't always have this belief. Women especially often don't. Plus it's possible to be promoted to a management job and not be given any training in "how to manage." You're expected to just do it. Yikes.

So here's what you need to know: When you manage people, you have two jobs. One is to accomplish the work your team is meant to do—run a restaurant, publish a magazine, learn English, whatever. The other is to *help your people achieve their potential.*

It's true. If you help your people be the best they can be, they in turn will do fabulous work for you and your organization. The best leaders serve their people, not the other way around. *The reason you need to know this is that remembering you are there to serve gives you the self-belief you need to assert authority.*

Here are fifteen more things to remember, and do:

- Be the boss. (You can be friendly, but you can't be a friend.)

- Recognize you will need to earn your employees' respect.

- Act the way you want your employees to act (honest, respectful).

- Spell out your expectations and goals.

- Provide the tools employees need to achieve the goals.

- Keep your word, even when it hurts.

- Praise in public; criticize (if necessary) in private.

- Take the time to listen to your employees. Really listen.

- Respect your employees' capabilities.

- As long as the job gets done, allow them to do it their way.

- Give your employees the credit when things go well.

- Step up and take the blame when things go wrong.

- Ask for feedback and respond to it.

- Consider your employees' needs, even if they're different from yours.

- Learn to delegate. Allow others to take the lead.

Most people want to do a good job. Your task is to help them. From there everything falls into place—a happy team, a job well done, and a fabulous future for you.

So where does that leave Working Girl's "I don't care if you lose your jobs" rant? It worked because it was a reality check. The men's behavior was over the top and they knew it. But a great leader—a great boss—never needs to rant. She leads with grace, class, kindness, and dignity. You don't become a great leader overnight.

Working Girl is still working on it.

Mary, (EX-) SUBSTITUTE TEACHER

"You know how kids always torture the substitute teacher. My survival trick, which I called 'defanging the wildcat,' was to pick out the most disruptive kid in class and turn him into my helper. I'd give him a responsibility, like taking attendance. I'd ask him to remind me of people's names (even when I knew the names). Making my adversary an ally gave me better control over the whole class."

day
care
drudge

Oh Baby

HERE'S A TALE TO MAKE YOU QUEASY. (Remember: It happened a long time ago.)

Place: Phoenix

Employer: A day care center

Job Duties: Mop floors, clean toilets, wash sheets, mind children

Note that "mind children" was last. The day care owner had funny priorities.

One afternoon, on her way to fill the scrub bucket, Working Girl poked her head into the toddler room. The room was clean but bare—no furniture, no curtains, no pictures, no TV, no toys. Just two- and three-year-olds parked on the linoleum floor.[*]

The children were crouching in a circle, heads down, voices low but animated. What could they be playing with? Working Girl, afraid it was a tarantula (not unheard-of in Phoenix), kicked through the child-proof gate and rushed into the room.

"What have you got there?" she cried.

The children scattered. There, on the floor, lay the objects of their fascination: Three hard little turds.

"Dickie did it!" announced one of the girls.

Dickie nodded proudly. And why shouldn't he be proud? He had done what the day care owner had not.

He had provided toys for the children.

Are you a new mother, pregnant, or planning to be pregnant? Do you need or want to keep your job? Is this kind of story one of your worst fears?

Welcome to the Work/Life Balance Nightmare, where it seems your only options are bad options:

---

[*]This was a very spare day care center that back then seemed less horrible than it does now.

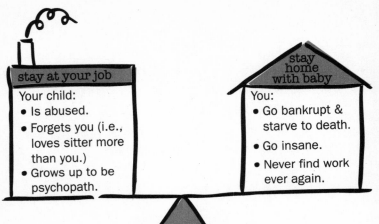

Working Girl is going to come straight out and say that she has never had children. But she feels that the motherhood/work issue is too huge to ignore. So, here goes:

Women in our modern society have more opportunities than ever. We are told we can be the fabulous career girl, the fabulous wife/partner, the fabulous mom. And we can.

The problem is we are told to be all these things simultaneously.

Balancing Baby & Boss—Nine Options

(You may have to try several different arrangements before you find the one that works. You may—no, will—have to change your arrangements as baby grows older.)

- Find *good* day care
- Hire a nanny
- Make arrangements with a relative
- Telecommute
- Work odd hours (i.e., flextime)
- Job share
- Work part-time
- Start a home-based business
- Take time off (& become super frugal)

! For every one of these options, you'll find experts who cite studies that prove you've made the right choice.

! For every one of these options, you'll find experts who cite opposing studies.

Not only that, but standards (for work and for parenthood) are getting higher and higher. It's maddening, because when the sky's the limit, not reaching the stars feels like failure.

Working Girl wants to tell you, please give yourself a break! A few suggestions:

- Accept that motherhood and anxiety go together like peanut butter and jam.
- Try to remember that children are resilient, that one bad experience (like, say, playing with poop) is not going to do permanent damage.
- Talk to other women balancing baby and boss—you're not alone!
- Keep in mind that, whether you're at work or at home, you can provide your child with a positive role model of a woman contributing her talents to the world.
- Remember that when you act out of love, you can't go far wrong.
- Finally, take a look at the options that exist for working moms (see chart above). You have more choices than ever before in the history of womankind.

The fact is that you, dear fabulous fellow working girl, *can* create a balanced, solvent, sane life that nurtures both you and your child—a life based not on guilt but on what works and on what makes you and your little one happiest.

The world is a much better place today. We know to put "mind children" in front of "mop floors."

Meaning: Have fun with that baby.

assistant manager

The Persistence Loop

a morality play in one act

(SETTING: THE FRONT COUNTER AT A HOUSE OF FABRICS STORE IN PHOENIX, AZ.)

Working Girl: "Um, hello. I was wondering if you had any openings."

Manager: "No, not right now. Come back next week if you want."

A WEEK LATER.

WG: "Hello. You said I should come back in a week."

M: "Oh. Still don't have anything. Sorry. Try again some other time."

A WEEK LATER.

WG: "Hi. I'm just checking back."

M: "You again. Have you filled out an application?"

WG: "No, not yet!"

M: "Well, here. Bring it back when you're done."

A WEEK LATER.

WG: "I brought back the application."

M: "Has it been a week already? The problem is, I don't have an opening at the moment. Why don't you come back another time?"

WG: "In a week?"

M: "Why not."

TWO YEARS LATER.

WG: "Hey, remember two years ago when I was trying to get a job here and you kept telling me to come back 'in a week'?"

M: "Ha. Yeah. I couldn't believe you kept coming."

WG: "But you said I should!"

M: "I was just trying to get rid of you."

WG: "Really? I thought you actually meant to come back. But you did end up hiring me."

M: "Yeah. I figured anyone who wanted to work here that bad would be a good employee."

WG: "Huh. Good thing I was too dumb to give up."

And that's how Working Girl got her best-ever college job at good old House of Fabrics.

You're thinking this chapter is all about how super-duper persistence is, right? Right. Persistence is a hugely useful life skill. (Note that word *skill*. Persistence isn't a trait you are born with or not born with. It is learned.)

ETERNAL TRUTH
Things seem impossible only until you do them.

Persistence is as important as talent or brains. A lot of the time you can make up what you lack in talent or brains by being persistent. In fact, all the talent and brains in the world won't bring you your heart's desire if you don't have the persistence to pursue that heart's desire.

Here's a biggie:

Persistence is the key to living an exceptional life.

The really good goals tend to be hard to get. We achieve those goals by being—you got it—persistent.

Yeah, yeah, yeah, it's easier said than done. The very meaning of persistence is "continuing to try even when you aren't succeeding."

When people say, "Be persistent," what they're really saying is, "Force yourself to keep on trying even when your efforts are failing and—oh, by the way?—we don't care how hard it is." You will have days, maybe lots of them, when you are ready to give up. Rejection and failure truly suck.

There is only one cure. When you are feeling at your lowest, your most miserable, your most defeated, do a tiny little thing that moves you toward your goal.

You will, correspondingly, feel a tiny bit better. Next step: Do another tiny thing. Hmmm, that feels good, too. So do another, maybe slightly bigger, thing.

That's the persistence loop. Action leads to success, which leads to more action. And more success.

SIX PERSISTENCE TIPS

· Break up your main goal into mini-goals, and your mini-goals into micro-goals.

· Do a micro-goal every day.

· Once a week, try something that scares you a little. This makes you stronger.

· Hang out with other people pursuing big goals. Support and help each other.

· Celebrate every time you attain a mini-goal.

· Welcome obstacles. Obstacles are how you know you're making progress.

JOB SURVIVAL TIP

Elaine, FINANCIAL ADVISOR

"When I decide to go after some big goal, the first thing I do is tell people—friends, family, colleagues. Then I ask them to ask me about it from time to time, so I know someone is holding me accountable. Plus, talking about the goal makes it clearer in my head and I may even change my mind about part of it. Most of the time, though, making it public reinforces my decision—I have to carry through or be embarrassed that I gave up. Telling people spurs me to pursue a goal even harder."

CAREFREE

translator

Looking & Leaping

PICTURE YOURSELF AS AN OLD LADY. "Old" as in in-a-rocking-chair-at-the-home-and-contemplating-your-life old.

What would you regret?

It's a good question to ask yourself when thinking about taking a chance on something that you really really really want, but that scares the willies out of you.

It's how Working Girl dared to move to Paris.*

She spoke high school-level French, had no job

---

* Why did she go to Paris? Because she knew it would make her happy. And it did, once she got the hang of it.

lined up, and knew exactly one person in all of Europe. Her first afternoon in the City of Light was spent lying on the bed in her dingy rented room and crying.

It took three months to find work, six to find enough work to live on.

What kind of work? Well, did you know that French companies need marketing materials written in English?

A perfect job for Working Girl, who despite her not-so-hot French was able to adapt French brochures into super-duper native-sounding American English.

The point? It was a job she never even knew existed. And she never would have found out it *did* exist had she continued to sit on her butt in Phoenix, daydreaming about living in Paris.

Sometimes the only way forward is in a direction that looks an awful lot like a jump off a really high cliff. The old-lady-in-a-rocking-chair test is a good one to apply when asking yourself, "Should I jump?" Here's some more help:

Risky Business Checklist
do any or all, in any order

- Identify what it is that's scaring you. It may not be what you think.

- Break down the big risk into smaller risks. Tackle them one at a time.

- Consider that in the long run not taking the risk might be scarier, or even more foolish, than taking the risk.

- Think of intelligent ways to minimize the possible downsides of the risk. Have money in the bank. Have a Plan B.

- Practice risk-taking. Learn to recognize successes. Learn to bounce back from failures.

- Hang out with bold, positive, courageous people who take risks in their own lives and who support your goals.

- List the things you need to take the risk (money, training, a mentor, a contact name, child care) and work to get them.

- Imagine the worst possible thing that could happen if you took the risk. Make a plan for dealing with it (you will probably never have to use this plan).

- Teach yourself to *welcome* fear as a sign that you're stretching yourself.

- At one point you will need to stop preparing and start acting, whether you feel ready or not (you won't). Close your eyes and jump!

JOB SURVIVAL TIP

Jean, NATUROPATH

"I started my career in the California school system. Then I quit to spend six years sailing around the world. Then I got a job at Microsoft. Then I quit and went to school to become a naturopath. Love it! I get the guidance and courage to make these huge life changes by 'accessing my inner voice'—through art, meditation, dreams, the I Ching, and even gardening. I've found there's no one path. You can get to where you need to go in many different ways."

English teacher

The Right Stuff

"I YAM WHAT I YAM, AND THAT'S ALL THAT I YAM."
Popeye the Sailor Man was lucky. He knew exactly
who he was.

Do you know who you are?

Don't laugh, not everyone does.

And, guess what, when it comes to jobs, you need
to know who you are and what you have to offer. It's
not obvious! Why do you think Working Girl has gone
through 59 jobs?

Part of the problem is that she was chronically desperate for money, so WG always took the first job that came along. For example, for an entire year she worked part-time for the French military, teaching English to French generals, colonels, ship captains, fighter pilots, and officers of the gendarmerie.

Her qualifications?

Zip.

No degree in education. No teaching experience. No language training of any sort whatsoever.

Even worse, Working Girl has a slight lisp. Several times a week she was appalled to hear one of her students perfectly reproduce her pronunciation of, say, "seashell."

"Don't say it the way I say it!" she would cry. But they never understood.

Lesson learned: A job that reveals your weaknesses and doesn't take advantage of your strengths is a formula for failure. The first trick is to figure out what your strengths are, and build on them (for the second trick, see "Work What You Got," page 184).

Working Girl, who does not believe things need to be complicated, has boiled down this process into six simple steps:

Turn the page. . .

Working Girl's 6 Simple Steps
to Self-Enlightenment
and Total Job Bliss

Step One: Take two sheets of paper.

Step Two: On Sheet 1, list your traits, good and bad. Energetic, disorganized, resilient, logical, clumsy, meticulous, lazy, imaginative, shy, savvy? What are you?

Step Three: On Sheet 2, make three columns and entitle them thusly:

- Traits I like and want to keep
- Traits I don't like and want to change
- Traits I don't like but am unlikely to change

Step Four: Take the traits from Sheet 1 and arrange them on Sheet 2 into the columns from Step Three. Be honest.

Step Five: Scotch tape completed Sheet 2 onto your bathroom mirror.

Step Six: When you need to make a big life decision, consult Sheet 2.

Does that college major, that job, that promotion, require a lot of traits from Column 1? Super.

From Column 2? Doable, if you are sincere about changing.

From Column 3? Beware.

The surprising thing is not that this is so simple.

The surprising thing is that even though it is so simple, hardly anyone does it.

P.S. If you ever meet a lisping French general, he was probably one of Working Girl's students.

Work What You Got

OKAY, YOU DID THE EXERCISE IN "THE RIGHT STUFF." You may be left thinking: Strengths good. Weaknesses bad. Right?

Hmmm. Maybe it's not as simple as that.

We like our strengths. We naturally gravitate toward jobs that match our best abilities and deepest interests. It's pretty much a no-brainer.

But our weaknesses are a part of us, too. Wouldn't it be nice if we could do something with them? Like, make them into advantages?

It worked for Working Girl.

"So, uh, we've got some documents that need editing," Prospective Client said.

"Cool," said Working Girl.

"I don't know if you're familiar with the subject matter."

"What *is* the subject matter?"

"Oil spills. Marine habitat."

"Um, okay," WG said, stalling. "Who's the audience for these documents?"

"They have to go to the public."

"Oh! So they need to be clear to the lay reader." Working Girl leaned back in her chair.

"Actually I don't know a single thing about oil spills in marine habitat," she said, "and that's my main advantage to you. It'll be easier for me to tell if something is confusing or unclear."

"Huh," Prospective Client said. "So you're saying that your main qualification for the job is that you don't know anything?"

"Exactly!" said WG. "Of course I know a lot about grammar. And syntax. And punctuation. But not so much about your subject matter. That makes me your ideal reader."

Working Girl got the job.

That, fellow worker bees, is called "reframing." You take a so-called weakness and look at it positively, from the employers' point of view. What matters most to them? What is the goal they're trying to achieve? It may just be that your unique combination of competence and incompetence is exactly what they're looking for.

Reframing is wonderful because it rewards you for both your strengths and your weaknesses. It's a step toward that major goal—authenticity (see "Get Real," page 229). Want to look stronger? Be honest about your shortcomings. It sounds counterintuitive, but admitting a weakness is a fabulous way to show strength. Often our first impulse is to hide our flaws. This never works. It's far better (not to mention easier) to be upfront about not only who you are and what you can do, but who you're not and what you can't do.

Does this mean you should never bother to try to fix your flaws? No, no, no! Working Girl would never discourage self-improvement! Facing a weakness— especially one that is only a bad habit, like tardiness or sloppiness—and turning it around is an important way to grow. Learning new skills and abilities is one of the joys of life. It would be a huge pity to deprive ourselves of that.

So study your weaknesses before deciding what to do with them. Some can be turned around. Some can be canceled out by finding a partner who is strong where you are weak, and vice versa. Some can turn into major advantages when put in the proper setting.

You are a package of strengths and weaknesses. We all are. If you ever find a job that calls for the whole package, as is—well, grab that job, baby, because it was made for you.

ETERNAL TRUTH

You achieve happiness by being more of who you are, not less.

kitchenware clerk

The Teeter-Totter

THERE'S WORK. THERE'S LIFE. How do you make the two fit together?

You will be solving this puzzle your entire career.

You won't get a lot of help. Employers talk about how they value "work-life balance," and maybe they mean it, but mostly it's going to be your task to create harmony between everything you do and everything you are.

How? By (a) figuring out your priorities and then (b) finding—or creating—a job that fits those priorities.

Here's a small-scale example: One day Working Girl

decided to get a night job. She wanted to work 20 hours a week, not including Saturdays, finishing up no later than 9 p.m. She wanted attractive surroundings, mindless work, and no management responsibilities (her day job was stressful enough). She didn't want a lengthy commute, so the place had to be either close to where she lived or close to the day job. She didn't want to be chained to a desk or standing in one spot all night—she wanted to be on her feet and running around.

Once she had her needs spelled out (as per "Moonlighting," page 72), her potential new employer was obvious: The upscale and nearby Diamond's Department Store. She applied. No openings. She waited a month and applied again. No openings. Two weeks later, she went back a third time.

"Why do you want to work here so bad?" the personnel manager finally asked.

Here was where WG was supposed to say something BS-y like, "It has always been my dream, since I was a tiny little girl, to work at Diamond's."

"Because it fits into my life," was what she really said, and got the job. She worked as a salesclerk in the kitchenwares department at Diamond's for two years.

Being clear on what you want and need is the first step toward approaching work-life balance. That's right, "approaching." Work-life balance is a continuing quest. You never really get there.

Think of a teeter-totter. The object isn't to achieve complete and permanent balance. It's to enjoy the ride.

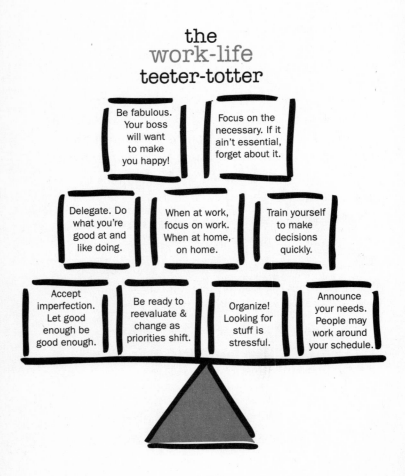

the
work-life
teeter-totter

Be fabulous. Your boss will want to make you happy!

Focus on the necessary. If it ain't essential, forget about it.

Delegate. Do what you're good at and like doing.

When at work, focus on work. When at home, on home.

Train yourself to make decisions quickly.

Accept imperfection. Let good enough be good enough.

Be ready to reevaluate & change as priorities shift.

Organize! Looking for stuff is stressful.

Announce your needs. People may work around your schedule.

Jennifer K., EDITOR

"I've got a more-than-full-time job, a husband, and a toddler. The way I stay balanced: At the end of every work day I take a yellow legal pad and my favorite pen (the one that makes my handwriting look better than it really is) and make a list of the tasks I need to tackle the next day. Then I get a paper towel and some spray cleaner and wipe all the dust and fingerprints and what- ever off my desk. I put the to-do list on the new clean surface. I go home relaxed and with a clear head."

corporate
minion

Playing
Like a Girl

WE WILL CALL HIM JOHN DOE.

"You're ruining our weekly meetings," said John.

"I am?" said Working Girl.

"We can't be ourselves."

"You can't?"

"The problem is that you're a woman."

"You didn't know?"

"None of us guys can relax. Meetings are no fun anymore."

He can't be serious, Working Girl thought. "You mean you want to be able to swear and fart and stuff?" she asked.

"Very funny. This is a real problem."

"Well, but is it *my* problem, or *your* problem?"

John swiveled in his chair to face the window. "Women in management," he grumbled. "Nothing's the same these days."

You're thinking this could never happen today, right?

Think again, kiddo.

The John Does of this world are not extinct. They continue to pop up everywhere. (Are they self-replicating? No one knows.) Your particular industry or the part of the country you work in may turn out to be a bastion of male chauvinism. And when you are the only woman in a workplace full of men? Testosterone alert!

What's a working girl to do? This is controversial, so hold on to your tutu:

> In a workplace full of guys, it helps to become a little bit like a guy.

Not entirely. You don't need to turn into a man to work with men. Yuck. But when you are functioning on your own in a guy universe, it can be enormously helpful to know and understand and at times observe these guy guidelines:

(WARNING: You are about to read a list of gross generalizations.)

#1 Guys say their most important point first. They don't build up to it, they just spit it out.

#2 Guys respect facts and data. When they can, they use numbers to back up their ideas.

#3 Guys don't mind fighting. If their suggestion is discounted or ignored, they restate it and try again. They don't complain no one is listening to them.

#4 Guys interrupt. They dive into conversations without invitation. They expect to challenge and to be challenged. They don't take stuff personally.

#5 Guys don't ask for directions! They think asking questions is a sign of weakness. They start in and hope they will figure things out as they go along.

#6 Guys don't care about details. They don't care how you do something, only that it gets done.

#7 Guys are results-oriented. They put more emphasis on the solution than on the problem.

Are you thinking, *Hey, I know plenty of guys who don't act like this!* Of course you do. People are individuals. Guidelines are just guidelines, even guy guidelines. But if you ever have trouble getting your job done when you're working with all men, try adopting some of these guy behaviors. You will be amazed at how effective they can be.

Hints: Use a relaxed tone of voice. Be assured and assertive. Keep your sense of humor. (You'll need it.)

JOB SURVIVAL TIP

Carla, CIVIL ENGINEER

"I supervise a road crew. Sometimes they'll try to intimidate me, like showering me with concrete for example. I learned early on to step away from the concrete! They're just trying to get to me. I never reward the bad behavior with attention. I continue to treat them like colleagues, even when they act like morons. And I never allow them to think they might be getting to me, even on days they do. Especially on days they do."

night
editor

Friends

YOU MAY MAKE FRIENDS AT WORK. YOU MAY NOT.

Working with friends is great. Working with friends makes you *want* to go to work. You may work longer hours, which could be good for your career. You may be more creative, and thus do better work, because you're happy.

Even more: Work friends watch your back and keep you sane. Work friends make a job more fun. Work friends may be the people who understand you the best because they "get" what you do all day.

However (there's always a "however"), finding a

true-blue friend-for-life at work is rare. Work friend-ships can feel like the real thing but—and this sounds sad but it's a fact—usually they last only as long as the job lasts.

Friendships at work are based on proximity (you grow accustomed to their faces). Or mutual self-inter-est (you scratch their backs, and vice versa). Or horrific work conditions (you unite against a common foe). Whatever. You are best buds as long as it's beneficial to both of you.

Enjoy it while it lasts.

After you leave a job, the Two Percent Rule kicks in (numbers entirely made up by Working Girl, but she bets she's right):

- 85 percent of the time, you never contact them and they never contact you;
- 10 percent of the time, you exchange holiday cards for a few years;
- 3 percent of the time, you get together every six months or so; and
- 2 percent of the time, you remain close friends.

Oh, and what about LOVE?

Yes, Virginia, people do date co-workers. Some people even meet their husbands/wives at work.

A Two Percent Tale

Key: WF=Work Friend, WG=Working Girl

R-r-r-r-i-n-g.

WF: "Hey."

WG: "Hey."

WF: "Would you like to edit the environmental impact statement I'm working on?"

WG: "Ummm. I don't know. I'm kinda busy."

WF: "I'm getting M. to do the word processing."

WG: "Really?"

WF: "Yeah, it'll be just the three of us again."

WG: "Remember last time?"

WF: "I do. Fun. Plus we can work at night."

WG: "Nice. When's the project due?"

WF: "End of the summer."

WG: "Short."

WF: "And sweet."

WG: "I could use the money . . ."

WF: "Yup."

WG: "I don't see how I can say no."

WF: "Of course you can't say no!"

(Conclusion: Working Girl worked all summer with good friends, earned a pile of money, and loved it.)

Dating colleagues is becoming more and more accepted (check your company policy!). But it still carries risk. Your boss may be less than thrilled. Coworkers are sure to tease you. And if love goes wrong, dealing with your ex on a daily basis could be excruciating. Worse, if your former beloved is the vindictive type, you could lose your reputation or even your job.

Still. Isn't L-O-V-E the most powerful force in the universe?

So try this: Make it a general policy to avoid dating at work. Avoid casual hookups. Be wary of temporary infatuations. Put up defenses. Erect barriers.

If the one who's caught your eye is The One, the attraction will outlast your defenses and crash through your barriers. Then:

Be cool. Continue to act professionally at work; do your job as well as (or better than) ever.

Be smart. Keep it a secret (but be prepared for the news to get out).

Be big. No smutty emails, no footsie in the boardroom, no quickies in the supply cupboard.

Be fair. If there's a potential for conflict of interest, ask to be transferred (or even get a new job).

Be wise. Do a prenup! Seriously—decide in advance how you would handle it if you break up.

Work is a great place to find friends and more. But be happy if all you find is a decent group of colleagues you enjoy and can get along with.

Hell Is Other People

THE FLIP SIDE OF WORKING WITH FRIENDS? Working with whiners, nitpickers, tattletales, finger-pointers, gossips, psychos, martyrs, saboteurs, thieves, and boss's pets. Not to mention brownnosers, busybodies, bullies, and backstabbers.

You'll encounter one or two along the way.

At a temp editing gig a few years back, Working Girl landed in a whole nest of them. Dick hated Jane. Sally wouldn't talk to Susie. No one met your eye. No one said "hello" when you arrived, or "have a nice evening" when you left. You had to sign over your

firstborn to get a ream of paper from the supply closet. There was even an evil email campaign to ruin the
reputation of a new employee.

Petty stuff. But enough to make you agree with
French philosopher Jean-Paul Sartre, who said, "Hell
is other people."[*] Even one aggravating co-worker
can make life at work next to unbearable.

Whaddya gonna do?

Bad co-workers range from a cubemate who steals
your stapler to a colleague who schemes to get you
fired. There's no one-size-fits-all solution. But here
are a few of the most common contentious co-workers and ideas for how to manage them:

The Backstabber. If someone circulates false-
hoods about you ("Sarah didn't finish her Friday
report till Monday"), correct the record immediately.
Be cool about it. State the facts. Move on.

The Saboteur. If someone takes a dislike to you
and delays, damages, or destroys your work, try doing
that person a big favor. Really. It's called "killing
them with kindness" and it works more often than
you'd think. At the very least it makes the person
look like a jerk if the sabotage continues.

The Dope. If an otherwise-okay colleague does only
one annoying thing, talk about it. ("I'm wondering if
you've noticed that . . . ") Most people don't know

---

[*] What he never knew is that other people said, "Hell is Jean-Paul Sartre."

they're driving you insane. Suggest a solution. Kindly.

The Needler(s). If co-workers attempt to bait you, or draw you into gossip, or whine to you, try deflecting them with humor. Or pretend you didn't hear them. Or find you suddenly have pressing business in another room. Whatever you do, don't get dragged down to their level.

The Unavoidable Pain. If you must work in close quarters with a severely disagreeable person, look for common ground (no matter how trivial—maybe you both like green Jell-O?). Don't waste energy hoping that person will change. It ain't gonna happen. But you may discover why the person is disagreeable (money, health, or family problems) and this may make it easier for you to deal.

The Psycho. If a co-worker seems set on destroying you (doesn't happen often, but it does happen), keep records of all incidents. Save emails. Print out blog posts. Take photos of the gossip written about you on the bathroom walls. Continue to do your job well. Keep your boss up to date on your performance and success. Be sure of your facts before bringing the issue to management or HR, and be ready to describe how you've tried to resolve the situation on your own.

Most of all, if a problem is one-time and petty, ignore it. Who cares who got the best chair? Don't expect people to be perfect, or to act the way you would. Recognize that not everyone at work is going to like you. Hard as that is to believe.

Oh, and remember to occasionally ask yourself, "Is it me?" Maybe your co-workers are as annoyed by you as you are by them!

ETERNAL TRUTH

No one is indispensable, but some people are a lot more dispensable than others.

Going Back to
Square One

SOMETIMES THE ONLY WAY TO TAKE A STEP
FORWARD IS TO TAKE A STEP BACK.

That's how Working Girl found herself working as a
receptionist. Now *that* was a hectic job. Men of all
nationalities crowded around her desk, clamoring for
attention.

"Mademoiselle! You have made a mistake! My sur-
name is spelled with two *a's*, not two *q's*."

Did WG mention the job was in Paris? More glamorous than Poughkeepsie, sure, but typing names on badges felt menial to her. (Hey—in her last job she had been a *manager.*) It didn't help that the men were demanding, and not that polite.

"Mademoiselle! I require a badge."

"Mademoiselle! You have omitted the hyphen in Jean-Louis."

"Mademoiselle! ——————"

You know what? Being a receptionist is a lot harder than it looks. But starting over often means starting at the bottom, and Working Girl really really wanted to live in France and the only way she could think to do it was to leave her corporate middle management job and go out to create a new life from scratch. Her receptionist gig at the Paris Air Show was her first job in France. It ended up being kinda fun.

You yourself may one day accept a position beneath your experience or expertise.

Maybe you left the workforce to have a baby, and when you came back you were told your skills were out of date. Or, your eyes on the prize, you determined that a downward move would give you the know-how needed for a much bigger job. Or you decided to change your life/career/place of residence and, like Working Girl, you had to start over at the bottom.

Whatever the reason, try to make the step-back

look like part of an overall life plan. Never change jobs out of fear or anger. Know what you want, specifically, before you move. Think it through (see "Looking and Leaping," page 176). It just may be that the step-back turns out to be the best thing that ever happened to you.

Then there is that other kind of demotion. You know, the involuntary kind.

Which happens more than ever. Used to be demotions were only for poor performance, but nowadays some companies use them as a cost-cutting tool. Others may even demote you to get you to quit (to avoid paying severance).

Getting kicked downstairs is stressful and humiliating. If it happens to you, here's what to do:

#1 Keep your cool. When your boss delivers the bad news (probably doing a poor job of it), don't show anger or say anything you'll live to regret.

#2 Find out why. You may never learn the whole truth, but once you've got your emotions under control, sit down with your boss and ask for honest, constructive feedback.

#3 Look inside. Maybe you need better skills, more education, a more positive attitude, a stronger work ethic. Maybe that job was just wrong for you.

#4 Look outside. Is your company in financial trouble? Are jobs in your field being outsourced? You may need to reposition yourself to stay on top of a shifting economy.

You might assume that the only sane response to a demotion is to resign. And that may be what you do. The key here is to make a rational decision. You always have the option of keeping or quitting any job. Choose wisely, in your own time, on your own terms.

One final thing to think about: We live in a culture where we are "supposed" to want position and power. But is that what you really want? Being queen bee has downsides. You may well be a happier person with a better quality of life and more job satisfaction at a worker bee job.

The truth is, most people's lives involve starting over at least once. It's kinda fun.

brochure writer

The Free in Freelance

IT WASN'T PLANNED. IT WAS PARIS.

Twenty of Working Girl's 59 jobs were freelance. Not because WG longs to be her own boss. But when she packed up her bags and moved to Paris she realized that if she wanted to eat and live indoors, she was gonna have to work independently.

First Thing She Learned: You never know where, when, how, or through whom you'll find a client. Parties, poetry readings, classes—potential work is everywhere. Be rational, cheerful, and punctual *always*, and you will impress someone enough to remember you.

Second Thing She Learned: Your competitors are not your enemies; they're the source of leads, support, and advice. As in:

R-r-r-r-i-n-g.

"Hello, Jack?" said Working Girl. "We met at the American Chamber of Commerce happy hour."

"Oh. Yeah."

"You mentioned you do freelance copywriting. I've got an offer to write a company brochure on chemical patents. How do I decide what to charge?"

"Ha. Glad you asked. Don't undercharge! Get paid what you're worth."

"But I don't know what that is."

"Here's what I do," Jack said. "I think about the job and ask myself, 'What is my rock-bottom price? What price would I hate myself for going below?' Then I triple it. Don't undercut the market. You'll hate yourself. And other freelancers will hate you, too."

Moral of the story: When you're freelance, your co-workers are other freelancers.

Freelance sounds fun—You get to set your own schedule! You can work at home in your bunny slippers! —but keep in mind that, especially in the beginning, you'll probably earn less than working a regular full-time job.

Plus you have to pay your own taxes, Social Security, and insurance. You need to have savings in case of lean times. You need to plan for your own retirement. You only get paid when you actually work (in a "real job" you can surf the web or chat with co-workers and still be on the clock). You have to be a dream employee, always proving your value to the client.

But freelance can be a wonderful thing. Here are more pluses and minuses to consider:

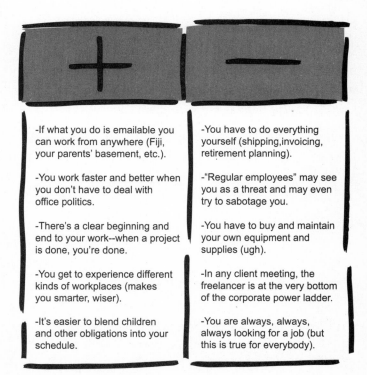

-If what you do is emailable you can work from anywhere (Fiji, your parents' basement, etc.).

-You work faster and better when you don't have to deal with office politics.

-There's a clear beginning and end to your work--when a project is done, you're done.

-You get to experience different kinds of workplaces (makes you smarter, wiser).

-It's easier to blend children and other obligations into your schedule.

-You have to do everything yourself (shipping,invoicing, retirement planning).

-"Regular employees" may see you as a threat and may even try to sabotage you.

-You have to buy and maintain your own equipment and supplies (ugh).

-In any client meeting, the freelancer is at the very bottom of the corporate power ladder.

-You are always, always, always looking for a job (but this is true for everybody).

Oh, and Jack's "triple it" system for determining fees? Working Girl used it the entire time she free-lanced in Paris. It worked like a charm. No one ever even asked her to lower her (tripled) fee. They just said, "D'accord," and paid up.

JOB SURVIVAL TIP

Marsha, WEBSITE DEVELOPER

"I allow myself to fire a client once a year. I generally say something like, 'I don't think our communication/work/art styles are a good match.' If they press me I tell them I don't feel I'm giving them what they need and I can't work like that. I recently did this to a potentially large client. It made me feel great. I did NOT start my own business so that I could work with people that make me crazy."

freelance typist

Title Schmitle

CLICKETY CLACKETY, WORKING GIRL LOVES TO TYPE. And she's good at it.

So, no surprise here, she's had a whole ream of jobs involving typing.

In fact, at one point she thought she would never get beyond clerical-level work, so she started telling new bosses she didn't know how to type. The ploy seemed to work, because right after that she started being taken seriously as a writer (ironic—because writers *type,* right?).

Image is important. Maybe too important. It's not

right, it's not fair, but we can be made to feel ashamed to be labeled a receptionist, or a mail-room clerk, or a typist, even though it is perfectly respectable work that needs to be done. There's an actual stigma: You can have an IQ of 150, but once the boss sees you as a clerical person you may always be a clerical person, at least at that company.*

Things are changing, though—not clerical jobs, or the bad rap given to clerical jobs. What's changing are the titles. You are no longer a receptionist. You're a Director of First Impressions. No more mail clerks—we now have Dispatch Services Facilitators. Typists? Try Digital Document Technicians.

It's called title inflation, and it's gotten out of hand. But it's harmless, right? Well, mostly. The trouble with overtitling is that it's confusing, and ridiculous, and no one is fooled. A weird title may make it harder for you to job hunt because it won't show up on search-es. This is especially true for the goofy titles you see at Internet start-ups. No potential employer is going to enter "Vice President of Cool" or "Chief Fulfiller of Needs" into a search engine.

And try going to salary.com and using your more-important-than-your-job title to find out how your salary measures up to others. Ha. You'll end up feel-

---

* Same stigma applies to lowish-level nonclerical jobs such as waitress, barista, salesclerk, etc.

ing underpaid. That's because you're comparing apples to oranges.

True, a title is a sign of importance. Your title reflects your status in a company. A good title can make you appear more credible to customers and co-workers. It may even make you do better work. While you're accepting a new job, you might want to negotiate a good title along with your good salary.

But keep in mind that a fancy job title costs an employer nothing. "Give 'em a title instead of a raise" is the oldest trick in the book! Don't attach too much importance to the words "manager" or "chief" or "senior" on your shiny new business card.

Years after Working Girl thought she had left all clerical work behind, she took on one more typing job. A company in Paris paid her four figures to type the text of an employee handbook into a computer. It took less than a week. Very, very worth it. WG was a typist again, but the money was easy and it was fast.

So go ahead and care about your title. But don't care too much.

JOB SURVIVAL TIP

Louise, SECRETARY

"I'm a secretary. Not a personal assistant. Not an executive assistant. Certainly not a 'Girl Friday'! The title 'secretary' has a long and dignified history; it refers to the person who is in on the secrets—and knows how to keep them. When the recent fancy titles have run their course, my prediction is that 'secretary' will make a comeback."

subcontract PR

Boomeranging

USED TO BE THAT WHEN YOU LEFT A JOB you
became *persona non grata* at that company. You'd
shown "disloyalty." Your name was mud. You were
dead to them.

Somewhere along the line somebody figured out this
was stupid, and today returning to a former employer is
so common it has a name—boomeranging.

Be a boomerang and you can:

Fly higher, faster. Leaving, getting valuable new
experience, and returning to your old company at a
higher level may scoot you up the corporate ladder

faster than if you'd just stayed and tried to rise through the ranks.

Negotiate better. One of the reasons companies like rehiring former employees is that it's cheaper than starting fresh with a new person. You already know the "company way." Remember this when negotiating your salary. Oh, and remember to get your old seniority and benefits reinstated—most corporations will do this.

Avoid the heartbreak of "résumé gap-itis." If you left the workforce for a while (to travel, to study, to have a baby), your past relationship with a company may make up for the gap in your work history. They know what you can do and love you for it.

(Um, they do love you, don't they? All of the above presumes you left on good terms. See "Quitting with Class," page 130)

Warning: While you're boomeranging, be careful you don't get clonked on the head. Be clear on the following: Why did you leave in the first place? What's changed (for the better or the worse) since you left? Is this a forward or backward career move? Could your former co-workers resent you and maybe even sabotage you? If so, how would you handle it? Are you only going back because it feels easy and safe?

Keep in mind that whoever said "You can't go home again" had a point. You've changed. They've changed.

It won't be exactly the same. If you've been away for a long time, or done such interesting stuff in your absence that you've grown beyond them, you may never be able to successfully return to a former life.

It happened to Working Girl. She rejected the so-called security of the corporate world to try her luck freelancing in Paris and has never been able to stomach a "real job" since.

She figured this out the minute she showed up for a meeting for a temp copywriter job in Seattle, post-Paris. Whoa. Déjà vu all over again. It wasn't just the cubicle farm stretching as far as the eye could see, or the cafeteria food stinking up the hallways at 10:00 a.m. It was the crushing atmosphere of apathy.

No one was in a hurry. No one was using an ounce more energy than necessary. Years before this job, Working Girl worked with a guy who by age 28 had already calculated what his pension would be when he retired in 37 years. That's what she felt in the corridors and elevators of this company. Hard to believe in this day and age, the employees were pacing themselves for the long haul. They had done the math and were waiting for life to begin—at age 65. Yeesh.

But you wouldn't do that, would you? You know that returning to a former employer, done properly, with your eyes wide open, for the right reasons, can be just the ticket. All you have to remember is that

when you let loose with that boomerang you should
be leaping forward, not stepping back.

bookkeeper

The Truth Will Set You Free

MONEY, MONEY, MONEY. Big bulging bags of fives and tens and twenties. Every morning Working Girl sorted it, counted it, bundled it, and locked it into the drugstore safe. Then she spent three hours trying to rectify the totals with the cash register receipts.

"They don't have to exactly balance," the manager had told her. "As long as they're within fifty dollars either way."

Fifty dollars??

The store had eight cash registers. If all eight

came out fifty dollars short . . . well, that was four hundred bucks.

Nearly three months' rent in those days. Enough to buy food for, like, a year.

Working Girl had her own key to the store. She came in before opening time to count the money. Alone. Who would notice if she helped herself to an occasional twenty?

At work, just as in real life, we get the chance to lie, cheat, or steal almost every day. Pilfering office supplies, calling in sick when you're not, embellishing your résumé, falsifying the number of hours you worked, padding expenses, taking credit for someone else's success—it's easy. Everybody does it.

Right?

Wrong. Not everybody. Only lame people. It's kinda sad. Lame people lie, cheat, or steal because they're afraid. They feel they have to be dishonest because everyone else is and if they're not, they'll be at a disadvantage. Or they feel they have to cover something up—a poor work history, a lack of education.

People also lie, cheat, or steal out of anger. They have a horrible mean boss. Or they didn't get the raise they deserved. So they feel the company owes them something and they talk themselves into believing it's okay to just take it.

As it happened, Working Girl was neither afraid nor

angry at her drugstore job. Because she was, as always, short of cash, she did sometimes visualize plucking a twenty-dollar bill from the pile and slipping it into her pocket. The manager probably wouldn't even care, she'd tell herself. After all, he was the one who'd hired Working Girl, not a real bookkeeper and only 19, to maintain his books. In a way, he was asking for it.

Nevertheless. It was just so low. Even thinking about taking a twenty gave her a dirty feeling. So while Working Girl has definitely not been an angel her whole life long (see "Do the Right Thing," page 69), she can point to *this* shining example of model behavior. She never took a cent. And today when she thinks back to that sort-of-bookkeeper job, she gets to feel like a winner.*

Here's how the game of life works:

Collect dirty feelings; you lose.

Collect great feelings; you win.

Need more reasons for being honest? How about:

· It's contagious. (Being honest with people means they're more likely to be honest with you.)

---

* Are you wondering if Working Girl ever did steal from an employer? Yes, she did. For a while, at a secretarial job in Washington, D.C., she snitched rolls of toilet paper from the ladies' room. It made her minuscule paycheck go a tiny bit further. But, yeah, she still feels bad about it.

- It's a sign of maturity and authenticity. (Earning you trust, respect, and other good things.)

- It keeps you out of trouble. (Duh.)

- It takes less energy. (Keeping lies straight requires a lot of effort.)

But the best reason for being honest is that it helps the world. And the world needs all the help it can get.

web writer

Keeping Up

YOU WENT TO SCHOOL FOR 13, 17, 19, OR MORE
YEARS. You should know a thing or two.

And you do.

Let's hope that one of the things you know is that
there's always something more to know. Not as obvious as it sounds! Many people assume that the
more stuff they do know, the less stuff they don't
know. And in a tiny way, this is true. But there is so
much stuff to know, plus new stuff being created all
the time. The universe of potential knowledge is a
really big universe.

Which means that the minute you start to think you know all you need to know, something like this happens:

A friend of a friend phoned. "Hey," he said. "I'm launching a website. Can you write some content for it?"

Working Girl has devoted her life to words. She's written articles, brochures, speeches, newsletters, press releases, annual reports, instructional manuals, and videotape scripts, plus other stuff she's forgotten. So she didn't hesitate. "Sure," she said.

Two hours later, she turned to her cat and wailed, "Oh my god, this is so much harder than I thought."

You doubtless already know what WG didn't. Website writing is a whole new kind of writing. Big learning curve here. Yeah, she did finally write that content, but the job took twice the number of hours she'd estimated. Hours she could not, did not, bill to the client.

However, she did get paid for those hours, in terms of new knowledge. New knowledge is fun, makes us more valuable as workers, makes us more interesting as human beings, keeps us from getting bored, keeps us from getting old, and is a path to discovering our true purpose in life.

Who can argue with that? No one, except the people who don't like new knowledge because it's a reminder they don't already know everything. And the people who aren't good at learning, or have forgotten how to learn, or are afraid to admit there are things they have yet to learn, or claim they don't have the time/energy to learn.

> **ETERNAL TRUTH**
> Believing you know everything is a sure sign of ignorance.

Fret not. Learning is a no-brainer. Babies do it. So when that learning curve starts to feel a little steep, come back to this chapter and take a look at these four super-simple tips for learning to learn:

Leave behind your ego. Being able to admit your ignorance is a sign of strength. When you don't know something, just say "I don't know. Could you explain it to me?"

Line up the things you don't know. Then rank them. You can't know everything about everything. Decide what you will learn in depth, what you will learn in breadth.

Link the old with the new. When faced with new information, connect it to something you already know. Ask yourself, "What does this remind me of? Where does it fit?"

Let go of the past. Unlearning is harder than learning. If you are able to part with ideas you mistakenly thought were true, you will learn new ideas faster and more easily.

People nowadays go on and on about how "lifetime learning" is a new phenomenon we have to master in this "constantly changing" world. But the fact is that throughout history there have always been lifetime learners, and lifetime learners have always been the happiest and most successful people on the planet.

Be one of them.

JOB SURVIVAL TIP

Stephanie, SALES EXEC

"A few years back my company offered French lessons to employees who were working with our French and Belgian clients. I signed up for them, but not just for my job. I did it for love. The classes were so much fun! I had a great time. Then, a year later, I was transferred to our Paris office. Not just because I knew some French. But it didn't hurt."

Get Real

HOW MANY OF YOU _ARE_ THERE? Depending on the time or place, you might be a worker, manager, owner, friend, neighbor, daughter, mother, sister, aunt, or girl-friend/fiancée/wife.

Your objective? To be the same person in all these roles.

It's called authenticity, baby, and it's a powerful career (and life) tool. Being authentic means that what you intend, what you say, and what you do are all the same. Authenticity saves you a lot of energy because you never have to "put on a face." On the job, being your authentic self means you're able to state your honest opinion and ask for what you need. What's wonderful about authenticity is that it frees you up to be more creative, intuitive, and innovative. At work, and everywhere.

There's more: Learn to connect with people in an authentic way and you will always have a job.

Here's how it worked for Working Girl. In Paris she scored a temporary gig attending meetings on behalf of a busy executive—a woman vice president for a technology manufacturer. She took notes and then briefed the VP. But then the weird thing happened. The series of meetings ended, yet Working Girl kept the briefings. The stressed-out VP had taken to using her as a sounding board and on-site friend.

Working Girl heard lots of juicy details about the VP's job, as well as her ex-husband, current (married) lover, daughter, house, and dog. And got paid $50 an hour for it. In return, the VP got WG's unbiased reactions and honest opinions.

When you are who you are, your special gifts reveal themselves. Working Girl's special gift is an ability to stay calm while others are freaking out. Sometimes that's all it takes to turn a work situation from ghastly to good.

What's more, when you are who you are, people will feel free to be who they are. Yes, authenticity is catching! Be a carrier and you will be valuable to have around. You may be worth $50 an hour, or more.

A word of caution: Some people think "being real" means you can do or say whatever you want. They say something thoughtless, do something selfish, and then announce, "This is who I am. Deal with it."

But authenticity isn't a weapon. It's not a license to criticize, insult, or offend. Blurting out something hurtful and calling it authenticity just makes you look like a jerk. Authenticity has to be balanced with kindness and an awareness of where people are coming from. Make it about them, not about you, and you can never go far wrong.

Authenticity needs to come from your heart, not your ego. When you are honestly authentic, you are someone people trust in and believe. That makes you a hot commodity, in the workplace and beyond.

middle manager

Take This Job and Love It

WORKING GIRL DID NOT ARRIVE AT AUTHENTICITY on Day One of her career. Stuff like this happened, even on Day Nine Thousand:

WG: "I'm leaving."

Soon-to-Be-Ex-Boss: "You're what?!"

WG: "I'm giving notice."

STBEB: "You've only been here five months!"

WG: "I know. I'm sorry. I've found a new opportunity."

Not entirely true. But at 37, Working Girl reached a now-or-never moment. She realized she had to either dump her PR career that very instant or work in a job where she felt unfulfilled, miserable, and frustrated forever.

"It's not right for me here," she added lamely.

Her STBEB didn't ask what the problem was. Nor did he point out that the company had just paid to move Working Girl all the way across the country for this management-level job. He looked, and probably was, angry.

"I'm sorry," Working Girl said again. She felt guilty and awful, but she had to go.

When you select a line of work, you're influenced by what's available, what you're naturally good at, what seems secure or prestigious or lucrative, and what your parents want. None of these may lead you to your true calling.

Finding your true calling requires all your energy, focus, commitment, time, work, talent, and love. It can take years and a lot of missteps. Probably will. No one offers you your life work on a silver platter. You have to find it, or create it, yourself.

The choice is yours! And it may be an unpopular one—if your mother is a neurosurgeon she may be less than thrilled about your decision to become a yoga teacher. But it's your life. Don't spend it living out your parents' dream. Live your own dream.

Here are a few tips for how:

TRUE CALLING DO'S AND DON'TS

Do know yourself. What makes you lose track of time? What fills you with energy?

Don't wait for a sign. Your calling normally does not come "in a flash." You have to search for it.

Do research. Who's living the way you want to live? Go talk to them. Read their blogs.

Don't wait for clarity. You may need to make a choice before you have all the facts. Dive in.

Do experiment. You may need to try more than one job. Take a chance.

Don't be afraid to undo a bad decision. It only hurts for a little while!

Do daydream. If you won the lottery or found out you had a year to live, what would you do?

Don't give up. Finding your true calling is a lifelong project (a fun one).

A huge sign that you've found your true calling is that you are a little bit afraid of it. There will be pleasure and pain—pleasure because you love it and it makes you happy, pain because the stakes are so high. When it's about your heart's desire, failure becomes scarier. You care. It's *your* work, *your* purpose. Own it.

At the same time, your true calling feels very right. It seems comfortable and inevitable. You don't mind the risks and problems, you make any sacrifices with joy, you are filled with energy.

Working Girl walked away from her respectable and okay-paying PR manager job and boarded a plane to Paris, where she had no job.

But within two years she was earning her living by writing. She had a string of clients. She was living in *Paris*. She was another step closer to her true calling.

(What's that? Writing this book for you, silly.)

JOB SURVIVAL TIP

Kristiina, EXECUTIVE COACH

"My experience has been that every time I give something up, leave something—even a job that I really like—I always find a much much better job than I ever could have imagined. That's my tip: Don't hang on. Let go. Take a risk. Our limits are self-made."

Waitress

How to Tell When You Are Successful

NO ONE DECIDES TO FAIL. But does that mean everyone decides to succeed?

Weirdly, no. Too often we don't take the time to define success for ourselves. We accept the commonplace definitions—fat paycheck, fancy title—without asking if those things are what *we* really want. And if you don't know what you want, how can you ever get it?

Picture a 12-table vegetarian restaurant in an up-and-coming neighborhood of Washington, D.C. Clean, well lit, smelling of cinnamon and fresh bread—a nice place for a night gig. And for Working Girl, part-time waitress, a 100 percent successful job.

That's because it had all four of the components of (work) success:

1. Mastery. Working Girl was a good waitress. She never dropped a plate, didn't mix up orders, and could calculate checks in her head. She was fast. On busy evenings she was faster—it was like floating. When you are good you know it and you get a charge from it. You don't need recognition (see "Praise Be," page 34). Nothing feels better, purer, truer, than doing something you are great at.

> A successful job is one you've mastered.

2. Money. How much money do you need to be a success? Simple—enough to make you happy. Working Girl's night waitress job boosted her from the ranks of not-quite-making-it to the ranks of a-little-more-than-making-it. That's the magic turning point at which money has a true, deep, and permanent influence on your happiness. Beyond the magic turning point, more money just equals more stuff. And as you may have figured out, the happiness you get from stuff is temporary.

> A successful job is one that pays you enough to live on, plus a little extra to save and a little extra for fun.

> **ETERNAL TRUTH**
> Money is funny. Once you have enough to take care of basic needs, it loses its power to make you happy.

3. Meaning. Health is important to Working Girl. So she relished serving healthy food—in this case, bowls of steamed organic veggies with brown rice—to hungry customers. It felt powerful and good. A job in line with your beliefs drives you, inspires you, and energizes you. You can feel positive about what you do every day, and that is huge.

A successful job is one that reflects your values.

4. Making a Difference. Working Girl, like you, would like to leave a legacy. Some jobs result in a permanent object that you can point to and say, "Here's what I did" (a bridge, a painting, a book). Others, like waitressing, don't. But wait. For all Working Girl knew, one of her veggie meals turned someone's life around. A pleasant smile, a good dinner—sometimes that's all it takes. We can never know for sure. What we do know for sure is that when you do your job well and with love, you add to the sum total of happiness in the world.[*] The world certainly needs that.

A successful job leaves the planet a better place.

We're told that success leads to happiness. But it's

---

[*] What? You worry your job isn't "good"? You wonder if your job might actually be harming your fellow humans and the planet? Go directly to "Do No Evil," page 142. And then to "Looking and Leaping," page 176.

the other way around. Happiness leads to success. Acing Mastery, Money, Meaning, and Making a Difference is where that happiness comes from. Leading you straight to . . . success.

A final cool thing about success is that once you've defined what it means to you, you can create it everywhere and anywhere. This is true of success in life as well as success at work. You can start succeeding at both, this minute, right away.

JOB SURVIVAL TIP

Tania, OPTOMETRIST

"When I was 14, my dad and I analyzed potential careers. We defined what I was good at (math, science, working with people), what I didn't want (unsociable hours, anything involving blood), and what I needed (flexibility, possible self-employment, decent earning potential early on). We hit on optometry. I have never met anyone who chose their career so young, in such an analytical way! But I was very happy with it. It felt tailor-made to me and turned out extremely well."

doughnut
girl

The Secret

"HEY! WAKE UP!" One o'clock in the morning and Working Girl's father was pounding on her bedroom door. "Your boss phoned. They need you to go in."

Huh? Working Girl had just gotten home from her evening shift. She'd been asleep for about five minutes.

"Are you up?" he shouted again.

"Yeah." She stumbled to the bathroom to check the uniform she'd washed out in the sink thirty minutes ago. Still wet. She put it on anyway, pulled her hair back in a ponytail, and left the house without making any noise.

Is hard work a good thing?

Working Girl's parents must've thought so. They let her work graveyard at Dunkin' Donuts when she was 16 and still in high school. In Working Girl's family, no one questioned the value of sacrificing sleep for a job. Even a kinda menial job like doughnut girl.

To this day, the odor of doughnuts makes Working Girl feel queasy. On the bright side, she learned this:

Hard work makes you resilient. Knowing you can perform gives you confidence. Confidence gives you the courage to take risks.

Hard work makes you powerful. When you become really good at a job you gain authority (whether or not you become the boss). Authority is power.

Hard work makes you stand out. Lots of people don't want to work hard. They never figured out the benefits (such as, fun).

Hard work makes you happy. It's absorbing. It's fulfilling. Working hard for something makes success, when it comes, very sweet.

Hard work is the link between wanting and having. If you're looking for The Secret, that's it.

It can be scary! Hard work leads to excellence, and excellence leads to success. Success is a threat because it involves change. A lot of people hate change. When you succeed, even people you thought were your friends may resent you or withdraw love.

Hard work, excellence, and success make you visible, so be ready to be seen.

Is it possible to work super hard and not get resilience, power, recognition, and happiness? Yup, it sure is. If you work like a demon at a thing you hate purely for financial, social, or professional security, you may get a big bad surprise one day (see "The Grand Illusion," page 45). Ditto for clocking in 80 hours a week because you're running away from something—a rotten home life, or no home life. And if you're doing the wrong kind of work (i.e., work other than your true calling) you can knock yourself out and still never be happy or feel like a success.

At this point in the book, you've realized that a big part of a happy life is working hard at work that is your true calling. Keep in mind you may not find your true calling the first year, or maybe even first the decade, of your working life. *Maybe* you will—but don't count on it. Meanwhile, the jobs you do along the way deserve your best effort.

And when you do find your true calling, remember this: Working hard doesn't mean just working long. It means working well.

Think efficiency. Smart working girls identify which tasks are important and which are just busywork.

Think innovation. Effective working girls know that ideas come when you take a break, step back, and look at your job from a distance.

Think courage. Brave working girls aren't afraid to question the status quo.

Be smart. Be effective. Be brave. Work well. Have fun. And don't forget to take a break every now and then and have a doughnut (and think of Working Girl).

stringer

Work as Play

YOU KNOW YOU'RE REALLY WORKING WHEN YOUR WORK FEELS LIKE PLAY. That's "play" as in engaging, exciting, and energizing. Work-as-play is a path to enlightenment. Really and truly.

Some people believe you're supposed to hate your job, that hating your job is a part of being grown-up. This is insane and sad. Work is a huge part of our lives and it can be a huge part of our happiness.

When Working Girl landed in Paris she got her first taste of work-as-play almost immediately. Go online and Google "Paris Voice." It's a monthly newspaper for English-speakers living in Paris. Like many another expatriate writer wannabe before and since, Working Girl wrote for the *Paris Voice.*

It was a revelation.

"Hey, Karen," said Bob, the editor. "A new Van Gogh museum is opening up. You wanna write a piece on it?"

Van Gogh? As in, the artist? Working Girl had spent the last 10 years writing about gas turbine engines.

"Wow," she said.

"Don't forget your camera," Bob added. "We'll need photos."

Really great work stretches you and shows you a bigger and more wondrous world than you ever knew was out there. In a small, baby-steps way, writing for the *Paris Voice* did that for Working Girl. She got to write about a fun, glamorous subject. She got to take photos and have them published. She got to create something that to her felt worthy and beautiful.

You'll know your work is play when:

- You are using all you know and all you can learn in the service of your work.
- You lose track of time when working because you're so in the present.
- You do even the icky parts of the job with resolve and willingness.

Your work is important because it's *you* made manifest. Act out of what is best in yourself and your work—and you—will become something wonderful. Pour love and energy and time into work and you can resolve your weaknesses, express your love, and learn who you are. Work is a friend that never deserts you and an endless source of energy and inspiration. Good old work.

So you're saying to yourself right now, "Yuck. My work isn't play. It's not a source of energy and inspiration. I hate my work."

Well, yeah. That's where you are right now. It's not where you're going to be forever. Your job, in addition to the one you're hating at the moment, is to put your two feet on the path to work-as-play enlightenment. It may take a while. But what else would you be doing?

Here's a big sign of wisdom: The ability to step back, look at your work objectively, identify its place in the world, and find the nobility in it. There's nobility in most every kind of work, including changing diapers, serving coffee, making photocopies, cleaning houses, and even writing about gas turbine engines.

Look for that nobility. You'll probably still hate your job, but you'll understand it better and feel better (even if only a little) about doing it.

Meanwhile, keep aiming yourself down the path toward work-as-play enlightenment. Do something every day that gets you a little bit closer (see "Take This Job and Love It," page 232). As long as you're moving forward, no matter how slowly, you're okay.

Getting Lucky

WORKING GIRL HOPES THAT SOMEDAY YOU WILL BE SO LUCKY as to have a position as great as "house Yankee."

Imagine a job in which your only duties are to (1) go to meetings, (2) look pleasant, and (3) be American.

The pay? Fifty bucks an hour. The location? Paris. The employer? A design consulting firm.

Apparently Europeans, even the French, believe that Americans are hard-working and effective in business. So when this employer pitched designs to clients, the boss believed it would look good to have an honest-to-goodness American on the team. Enter Working Girl, red-blooded female Yankee Doodle Dandy-ette.

Would you like to be lucky enough to fall into cool jobs like this one?

You can be.

We're used to thinking of people as either naturally unlucky or naturally lucky, but the truth is that luck is a learned ability.

The key is your behavior.

Do you fixate on your mistakes ("I knew I couldn't do it")? You will tend to attract misfortune. Do you shrug off setbacks ("Oh well, that didn't work")? Luck will come to you.

If you are so busy focusing on what you think you want, you will miss opportunities (bad luck). If you are relaxed and open, you will notice the opportunities actually out there (good luck).

> Just tell yourself, Duckie, you're really quite lucky!
> Dr. Seuss

Here's a surprise: Lucky people *fail* a lot more than unlucky people because they try so many things, thus increasing their odds of success. So try a lot of stuff. When you do succeed, as you will, people will forget the failures and say, "You're so lucky!"

Finally, lucky people know that Luck Comes Last.

You get it after the education, the training, the good attitude, the hard work, and the try-try-try.

Good luck!

Learning to be Lucky

1. be good at what you do
2. work like mad
3. put yourself out there
4. be willing to shift directions
5. listen to your intuition
6. be open to suggestions
7. don't freak out when you fail
8. expect to be lucky
9. be grateful when it comes
10. when it goes, let it go

Doing the Butterfly

NOWADAYS WHEN PEOPLE ASK WORKING GIRL
what she does, she says she is an artist.

Not a Picasso-type artist, oh no. She draws cartoons
(you've been looking at them all through this book).
Simple art, but art that people actually pay money for.*
This new career comes as a complete surprise to
Working Girl, who never used to be able to draw a
straight line, much less a curve, and who always
thought of herself as more of an analytical word person.

* As well as being the illustrations for this book, the cartoons are the basis of a
line of products called Another Working Girl.

But now she's "done the butterfly"—transformed from a hairy little caterpillar into a . . . you know.

Who are you? How would you describe yourself? Are you happy with this description? Most important, are you today the person you were meant to be?

Maybe not. A lot of us get shoved around by life. Responsibilities, mistakes, expectations, and fears send us off on paths we now see are wrong for us. Or keep us on paths that are suffocating our spirits.

The good news is that it's never too late to start down a new path, your true path.

Oops. Are you saying, "But I don't know my true path! I only know that the one I'm on is not the one I want!"

News flash: Few of us start out life knowing our true paths. You're probably gonna have to look for yours.

Tips for Discovering Your True Path
(do any or all, in any order)

#1 Notice what you notice. What makes you stop in your tracks, what gives you joy, what fills you with energy and excitement when you see it? Machines? Flowers? Children? Numbers? Words? Skyscrapers? Cows?

#2 Research. Books, magazines, the Internet—there's tons of self-help stuff out there! Take the tests, do the exercises.

#3 Remember. Think back to when you were little. Who were you then? Ambitious, fearless, stubborn, creative, meticulous, daring, fun? You are still that person.

#4 Go shopping. No, not that kind. Shop for a new life! Volunteer in new (to you) fields, talk to people living lives that interest you, travel, take classes.

#5 Write. If you are a word person, you should journal. Just sit down and start writing. No stopping, no self-editing. You may find yourself writing down the blueprint for your new life.

#6 Talk to a professional. A good job or life coach, a counselor, a clergyperson can serve as a sounding board, critiquer, and cheerleader.

#7 Go on a trip all by yourself. You will be away from everything that's keeping you stuck where you are, and you'll have a big block of time to notice, remember, write, etc. In unfamiliar surroundings you are more free to think unfamiliar thoughts.

#8 Imagine. You win the lottery, inherit $5 million, Bill Gates adopts you, your ship comes in. How would you use your new time/money? Seriously.

After you've bought the car, the house, and 50 pairs of shoes, what would you do with the rest of your life?

#9 Meditate. Pray. Contemplate. Reflect. Set aside some time every day to slow down and listen to yourself think.

Now comes the hard part. Once you have discovered your true path, you have to put both feet on it and start moving. It takes work. You will get discouraged, scared, tired, fed up, surprised, confused. Obstacles will pop up from the most unexpected places. You will feel as if you can't possibly succeed, no matter what you do.

You know what Working Girl is going to say, don't you?

#1 Keep trying.

#2 Keep on trying.

#3 Read the next chapter—"Your Mission Statement."

Oh, and one more thing: The hard part is in many ways the fun part. Some of the surprises will be good. (Working Girl did not see the artist thing coming—truly.)

Here endeth the 59 jobs.

Your Mission Statement

EVERY WORKING GIRL NEEDS A MISSION STATEMENT.

It's what helps us achieve our unique purpose in life.

Are you on your very first job and thinking it's a tad early to establish your grand "purpose in life"? Are you well into a career, knee-deep in job, babies, and mortgage, and exclaiming, "I don't have time to shave my legs, much less think about a mission!"?

It's not too early. It's not too late. It doesn't have to take huge blocks of time.

Working Girl bounced around for years, accepting any old job, changing employers for an extra nickel an hour, pouring energy and time into work she despised, trying to fit into the Corporate Career Girl mold, floundering through freelance. If there's one thing she learned, it's that if you don't take charge of your life, something else will.

Your Purpose in Life

So. You should take charge. How? Plenty of systems are out there, but here is the method that Working Girl developed, after much trial and error.

First rule is to start right away.

Second, go back and reread the last chapter, "Doing the Butterfly." Those tips for discovering your true path are going to come in real handy here.

Third, review the lists you made in "The Right Stuff," page 180. They'll get you started.

Fourth, pick up a pen, missy! Using all you've learned about your true path and who you are—so far—do these three things:

#1 Name your talents.

#2 List your values.

#3 Describe the kind of life that lets you use those talents and work toward those values.

Yikes. Too abstract? Let's get more concrete. Pick up that pen again and fill in the blanks of this sentence:

By the time I am_____ (age), I want to be living in_____ (place), doing _____ (things you like to do and are good at) _____, associating with _____ (people), helping them to _____ (their needs, wants, desires).

Take a look at the sentence you've just created. In it are your talents and values, expressed in a way that reveals your mission in life and suggests the steps you need to take to get there.

Here are some samples. See how filling in the blanks practically writes a blueprint for these four goals?

- By the time I am 30, I want to be living in a big West Coast city, developing computer software, associating with other computer geeks, helping them to create the next big killer app.

- By the time I am 30, I want to be living in a Midwestern small town, playing my guitar, associating with children and parents, helping them to love music as much as I do.

- By the time I am 40, I want to be living near the Pacific Northwest mountains, doing science, associating with other scientists and the public, helping them to preserve our natural environment.

- By the time I am 40, I want to be living on the North Atlantic seaboard, writing, cooking, and painting, associating with family and friends, helping them to love life as much as I do.

Don't worry if it takes you a while to complete your own sentence. It's short. The shorter a sentence is, the harder it is to write. But keep at it.

Hint: It gets easier the more you try it.

Some More Hints

Be specific and concrete. Be concise—keep your sentence to around 30 words. Be ready to revise and change—your mission statement evolves as you do. In fact, your mission statement may drastically change as you go through life. This is very normal.

> Feel free to be delusional. People who see themselves as smarter, luckier, better than they really are achieve more, because . . . they don't know they can't do it!

Then write it down and stick it on the refrigerator.

But don't make it too permanent. Because from time to time you are going to rethink and rewrite your mission statement. Aim to do this once a year, like on your birthday.

Ready to Act!

No, you are not done. Next step: *Start doing something every single day* that brings you closer to your mission.

You heard it right. Every single day. Sound impossible? Well, here's one very simple act you can do every day. You can save five bucks.

One way or another, your mission is going to call for cash. So decide on a specific amount and stash it away every single day.

> ### THE MAGIC OF COMPOUND INTEREST
>
> If you start saving $5 a day at age 20 and average 5 percent interest, by age 65 you'll have $356,446.26!
>
> (Oh boy, does Working Girl wish she'd known this when she was 20!)

Never let a 24-hour period go by without putting aside some money! Even if it's only a dollar. Even if it's only a quarter.

Step by Step by Step

Meanwhile, break down your mission statement into small, doable goals. Make a list of them in the order they will need to be done, so when you achieve one mini-goal, you have another one all ready to start on.

Feeling overwhelmed? Here are some sample mini-goals:

- enroll in a course
- join an online community

- volunteer
- research new jobs
- build a website
- read
- interview an expert
- start a blog
- go to the library
- ask for that promotion
- perfect your music or art or science
- offer to take on a new responsibility at work
- form a community action group
- take a trip to the place you want to move to

These are all concrete, doable actions that move you from Point A to Point B.

You've probably already guessed that each of these mini-goals can be broken down into even smaller activities (micro-goals).

For instance, interviewing an expert in the field you dream to work in involves:

- finding out who that expert is
- phoning or writing the expert to introduce yourself
- preparing for the meeting
- going to the actual meeting

- writing a thank-you note afterwards

Aim to accomplish a couple micro-goals every week, every day if you are really hot. The more micro-goals you achieve, the easier it gets and the more wonderful you feel.

Still Feeling Overwhelmed?

Remember, you are not in this alone!

Here's an idea: Form your own personal Board of Directors. This is a group of people (friends, family, teachers, bosses) who care about you, want you to succeed, and can help you. Your Board of Directors will give you advice, make suggestions, tell you when you've gone off track, listen to your ideas, rants, complaints, and fears, and give you a kick in the butt when you need it.

You can have as many people as you want on your board.

Have a lot so you don't wear out any one person.

The Most Important Part

That's basically it—yes, the secret of success! revealed here!—but other stuff will come up.

Expect failure and setbacks (see "The Persistence Loop," page 170). Don't be too stubborn to change course when it becomes clear something is not working. Recognize that it's scary to achieve your heart's desire, so you will feel fear, even panic, as you work through the micro- and mini-goals.

Oh, one more thing. This is really important.

You should be loving the process.

It may take you years to get to where you want to go. Maybe even decades. Meanwhile, you will be living your life. And you want to be enjoying it, not feeling you are giving up happiness-in-the-now for some faraway goal.

If you are not loving the process, take another look at your mission statement—something needs to be adjusted.

The world needs you, dearest fellow working girl. Striving toward the thing you were put on this earth to do is the most exciting, fulfilling, and wonderful way to live your life.

It's the only way to live your life.

You can do it.

APPENDICES

The Table of Contents by Subject Matter

CONFIDENT

The 59 Jobs in Chronological Order

(also, location)

#	Job	Where	When
1	Paperboy	Plainview, Minnesota	1962
2	Housecleaner	Phoenix, Arizona	1965
3	Filing mouse	Phoenix, Arizona	1965
4	Dishwasher	Phoenix, Arizona	1966
5	Nanny	Phoenix, Arizona	1967
6	Daycare drudge	Phoenix, Arizona	1967
7	Burger girl	Phoenix, Arizona	1968
8	Doughnut girl	Phoenix, Arizona	1968
9	Cigarette girl	Phoenix, Arizona	1969
10	Bookkeeper	Scottsdale, Arizona	1970
11	Cashier	Tempe, Arizona	1970
12	Envelope sorter	Tempe, Arizona	1971
13	Envelope addresser	Scottsdale, Arizona	1972
14	Seamstress	Tempe, Arizona	1973
15	Pollster	Tempe, Arizona	1973
16	Assistant manager	Phoenix, Arizona	1972—74
17	Night manager	Phoenix, Arizona	1974
18	Teller	Phoenix, Arizona	1974
19	Christmas temp	Phoenix, Arizona	1974

20	Store assistant	Arlington, Virginia	1974
21	Secretary	Washington, D.C.	1975—79
22	Hostess	Washington, D.C.	1975
23	Night typist	Washington, D.C.	1975
24	Waitress	Washington, D.C.	1976—78
25	Clerk typist	Phoenix, Arizona	1979—81
26	Busboy	Phoenix, Arizona	1979
27	Store clerk	Phoenix, Arizona	1979
28	Kitchenware clerk	Phoenix, Arizona	1980
29	Junior PR girl	Phoenix, Arizona	1981
30	Newsletter editor	Phoenix, Arizona	1982—87
31	Receptionist	Le Bourget, France	1987
32	Ditch digger	Harrachov, Czechoslovakia	1987
33	Foundry writer	Waterford, Ireland	1987
34	Corporate minion	Phoenix, Arizona	1987—89
35	Middle manager	Morristown, New Jersey	1990
36	Model	Paris, France	1990
37	Freelance contributor	Paris, France	1990
38	English teacher	Rochefort, France	1990—92
39	Stringer	Paris, France	1990—91
40	Marketing writer	Asnieres, France	1991
41	Consultant	Paris, France	1991

42	Researcher	Paris, France	1991
43	Freelance typist	Montrouge, France	1991
44	Brochure writer	Paris, France	1991
45	House Yankee	La Defense, France	1991—92
46	Confidante	Paris, France	1992
47	Freelance journalist	Paris, France	1991—92
48	Translator	Paris, France	1991—92
49	Disciplinarian	Versailles, France	1993
50	Subcontract PR	Tacoma, Washington	1994
51	Writer for hire	Redmond, Washington	1995
52	Document manager	Kirkland, Washington	1995—97
53	Night editor	Seattle, Washington	1998—99
54	Temp editor	Ballard, Washington	2000
55	Proofreader	Kirkland, Washington	2001
56	Web writer	Kirkland, Washington	2002
57	Editor	Bothell, Washington	2003
58	Scientific editor	Redmond, Washington	2004
59	Artist	Kirkland, Washington	2005—09

. . . and now (Job #60), author of THE AMAZING ADVENTURES OF WORKING GIRL: Real-Life Career Advice You Can Actually Use.

A DISCLAIMER

The author is not an expert in the field of work. Or in any other field.

She possesses no academic credentials that might indicate her suitability to dispense advice. She holds one undergraduate degree, a BA in political science, which as far as she can see does not qualify her for any professional or even remunerative activity.

All sidebars, charts, diagrams, and statistics were made up.

All illustrations were drawn by the author. She did not "get them out of the computer" as many persons have presumed.

All names have been changed or otherwise disguised. Persons whose past behavior does not now reflect well on them will know who they are.

Any grammatical, orthographical, or syntactical errors found in the prose of this book were somehow inserted after the manuscript left the editors' hands.

Persons wishing to take exception to advice in this book may address themselves to the author's agent, who has agreed to misplace such correspondence.

Working Girl Answers the Question:

Why So Many Jobs?

#1 Because they were there.

#2 Because she is easily bored.

#3 Because working for money is easier than worry-ing about money.

#4 Because sometimes she leaps before she looks.

#5 Because, in a weird way, she likes to work.

#6 Because some jobs are really bad, and when a job is really bad the only thing you can do is quit and find another one.

#7 Because we should embrace change.

#8 Because she does not define herself by her work.

#9 Because she does define herself by her work.

#10 Because the grass is always greener ... elsewhere.

Working Girl answers the question:

Why Working "Girl"?

(I.e., why not "Woman"?)

#1 Because Working Girl started work early.
When she was, you know, a girl. It stuck.

#2 Because Working "Girl" makes people
think of sex. Everyone likes sex.

#3 Because the two w's in "Working Woman"
make a disagreeable woo-woo sound.

#4 Because political correctness is such a drag.

#5 Because it's okay when we call ourselves girls.

#6 Because "Girl" is friendly.

#7 Because "Girl" is sassy.

#8 Because "Girl" is fun.

#9 Because "Girl" is memorable.

#10 Because that's the way it is.

Acknowledgments

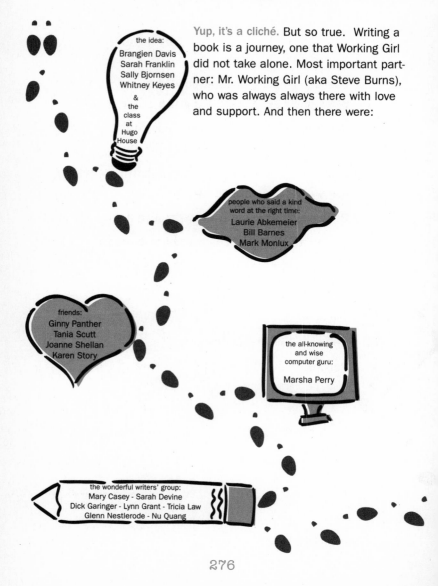

the idea:
Brangien Davis
Sarah Franklin
Sally Bjornsen
Whitney Keyes
&
the
class
at
Hugo
House

Yup, it's a cliché. But so true. Writing a book is a journey, one that Working Girl did not take alone. Most important partner: Mr. Working Girl (aka Steve Burns), who was always always there with love and support. And then there were:

people who said a kind word at the right time:
Laurie Abkemeier
Bill Barnes
Mark Monlux

friends:
Ginny Panther
Tania Scutt
Joanne Shellan
Karen Story

the all-knowing and wise computer guru:
Marsha Perry

the wonderful writers' group:
Mary Casey - Sarah Devine
Dick Garinger - Lynn Grant - Tricia Law
Glenn Nestlerode - Nu Quang

the fab four at Running Press:

Jennifer Kasius
Amanda Richmond
Donna Stonecipher
Melissa Appleby

great photos by Anne Lindsay

friend
mentor
Alice Acheson
saint
maven
publicist

more friends:
Elaine Chan
Zita Gustin
Melissa Wadsworth
Amanda Ford

the best literary agent in the universe:

Betsy Amster

Working Girl lives in fear that she forgot someone
Was it you?
If so, please write your name here:

and give WG a call.
She will make it up to you, somehow.

Index

Notes

Notes

Notes

Notes

Notes

Notes